Other Carver resources:

Boards That Make a Difference: A New Design for Leadership in Nonprofit and Public Organizations, Second Edition

The CarverGuide Series on Effective Board Governance (12 guides)

Board Leadership: A Bimonthly Workshop with John Carver

John Carver on Board Governance (video)

Empowering Boards for Leadership: Redefining Excellence in Governance (audio)

The Jossey-Bass Nonprofit and Public Management Series also includes:

Achieving Excellence in Fund Raising, *Henry A. Rosso and Associates*

Board Overboard, *Brian O'Connell*

The Board Member's Guide to Fundraising, *Fisher Howe*

The Board Member's Guide to Strategic Planning, *Fisher Howe*

Welcome to the Board, *Fisher Howe*

Governing Boards, *Cyril O. Houle*

The Drucker Foundation Self-Assessment Tool for Nonprofit Organizations, *The Peter F. Drucker Foundation for Nonprofit Management*

The Jossey-Bass Handbook of Nonprofit Leadership and Management, *Robert D. Herman and Associates*

Marketing Nonprofit Programs and Services, *Douglas B. Herron*

The Leader of the Future, *Frances Hesselbein, Marshall Goldsmith, Richard Beckhard, Editors*

The Organization of the Future, *Frances Hesselbein, Marshall Goldsmith, Richard Beckhard, Editors*

Nonprofit Boards and Leadership, *Miriam M. Wood, Editor*

Changing by Design: A Practical Approach to Leading Innovation in Nonprofit Organizations, *Douglas C. Eadie*

Strategic Planning for Public and Nonprofit Organizations, *John Bryson*

Human Resource Management for Public and Nonprofit Organizations, *Joan E. Pynes*

Secrets of Successful Grantsmanship: A Guerrilla Guide to Raising Money, *Susan L. Golden*

Fund Raisers: Their Careers, Stories, Concerns, and Accomplishments, *Margaret A. Duronio, Eugene R. Tempel*

Rosso on Fund Raising: Lessons from a Master's Lifetime Experience, *Henry A. Rosso*

Reinventing Your Board

Reinventing Your Board

A Step-by-Step Guide
to Implementing Policy
Governance

John Carver

Miriam Mayhew Carver

Jossey-Bass Publishers • San Francisco

Jossey-Bass Web address: http://www.josseybass.com

 Manufactured in the United States of America on Lyons Falls Turin Book. This paper is acid-free and 100 percent totally chlorine-free.

All policy samples © John and Miriam Carver.

All drawings © John Carver.

Policy Governance® is a registered service mark of John Carver.

Library of Congress Cataloging-in-Publication Data

Carver, John.
    Reinventing your board : a step-by-step guide to implementing policy governance / John Carver, Miriam Mayhew Carver.
        p.   cm. — (The Jossey-Bass nonprofit and public management series)
    Includes index.
    ISBN 0-7879-0911-4 (acid-free paper)
    1. Directors of corporations.   2. Corporate governance.
I. Carver, Miriam Mayhew.   II. Title.   III. Series.
HD2745.C3727   1997
658.4'22—DC21   97-4810

HB Printing   10 9 8 7 6 5 4 3   FIRST EDITION

The Jossey-Bass Nonprofit
and Public Management Series

Contents

Policies

Chapter Four

Chapter Five

Chapter Six

Chapter Seven

Figures

Chapter Eight

Preface

Since you have picked up this book, chances are that you and your board want to use Policy Governance to bring your organization to new levels of achievement.

Perhaps you were initially frustrated because the very concerns that led you to be on the board in the first place were the ones seldom discussed. (We have met countless school board members who were confused because they rarely talked about children, and members of hospital boards who rarely discussed the health of the community.) Perhaps you have already made gestures toward implementing Policy Governance but have simply needed more guidance on how and where to begin.

Congratulations! Contemplating a radical change in the way your board works is a brave step. This book is your guide to the application of a robust new governance model to your board.

We will assume you realize that Policy Governance offers a powerful approach to governance, one that is conceptually whole and oriented toward obtaining results for people rather than promoting organizational busy-ness. But because Policy Governance flies in the face of so much received wisdom and tradition, old habits may be hard to overcome. Wouldn't it be nice to start at the beginning with a brand new board, doing it all right from the start? But yours is an ongoing organization, perhaps with a rich tradition; your organization is also weighed down with structures already in place, ways of doing business that are hard to change, and personalities wed to old ways. You want to be a board that makes a difference, but you fear that implementing Policy Governance in a going business may be as complex as changing an airplane from propeller-driven to jet in mid-air.

We believe that board members don't have time to waste. We believe that they want to make a difference. We believe that the board has a real, not a ceremonial, job to do. And we are sure that the system of governance used traditionally in our nonprofit and public organizations is inadequate to provide boards with the skills and mechanisms they require to be effective leaders.

In 1990, the senior author, John Carver, wrote *Boards That Make a Difference* (Carver, 1990), a book that exposes the shortcomings of traditional governance and that substantially redefines the job of the board. The Policy Governance model, as he called his new design, has become widely known, and many boards have begun to implement its principles. Since implementing Policy Governance involves developing a newly defined type of policies, getting board commitment to act according to those policies, and delegating to a CEO in a new and exciting way, the board room and our concept of the board's job are extensively altered. With a change this big, it is no wonder that most boards need to secure help in moving forward.

Here it is! This book gives practical advice and assistance to your board in the process of making the change. It provides concrete policy examples for consideration and debate, and it offers practical counsel for the maintenance of the new system.

While this book does contain a brief description of the theoretical principles of Policy Governance, you will find that you can get more use out of it if you have already read *Boards That Make a Difference*. Since we are undertaking to assist in the implementation of a theoretical framework, knowledge of that framework is important.

The most difficult part of implementing John Carver's Policy Governance model is reaching a board resolve to follow *any* model. Boards have long been used to discussing anything that anyone wants to discuss, delegating the same job to more than one person, monitoring with no criteria to judge against, and failing to clarify the most important organizational value of all—the *purpose* of the organization.

If you want your board to achieve meaningful accountability for its organization, these habits and more must change. Your inquiry into Policy Governance is the first step to achieving these changes. If you are interested in rhetoric—new jargon but nothing new in action—put the book down. If you and your board are ready for an adventure in governance revitalization, read on. Here goes!

How to Use This Book

We have divided this book into three parts, each addressing a different phase of making Policy Governance work. To a great extent, you can jump about in the book, not following the sequence in which we present it. But regardless of the sequence you follow, understanding the way we have elected to put the material together will help you.

Part One

Part One gets you ready to begin. In Chapter One, we deal with some of the common queries boards raise prior to starting their Policy Governance implementation. In Chapter Two, we review the key theoretical principles of the Policy Governance model. This will assist you in your policy development work but will not replace the thorough understanding that results from reading *Boards That Make a Difference*. Chapter Three explores some of the implications of implementing Policy Governance for your board and staff.

Part Two

Part Two deals with the core of Policy Governance: the creation of a set of policies so conceived and so crafted that they can bear the full weight of board leadership of your organization. These are unlike policies as traditionally conceived, so they must be developed from scratch. You cannot simply adapt previous board policies for this purpose. In Chapters Four, Five, and Six, respectively, we take your board in step-by-step detail through the development of your Executive Limitations, Governance Process, and Board-CEO Linkage categories of policies. Throughout these chapters, we use sample policies in order to make the process go more quickly for you. Chapter Seven tackles the more difficult creation of Ends policies. Because organizations differ so greatly in their Ends, we use a series of exercises rather than samples for this final chapter of Part Two.

Part Three

Part Three completes the book by addressing what comes after the initial policy development. In Chapter Eight we discuss board documents as used by a Policy Governance board. The documents most familiar to boards today are certain to change, for they are based on old ideas of governance. Chapter Nine answers the frequently asked question, What do we do now? by suggesting issues you should consider in moving from your present governance style to Policy Governance, including relationships with stakeholders and methods of keeping your board on-track.

We are pleased to be able to work with you in the following chapters in preparing for change, in careful crafting of board policies in the new form, and in bringing a powerful coherence to the practices and documents of board leadership. As your board follows the steps we outline, it will be engaged in transforming its capability to govern, in nothing less than reinventing your board.

Atlanta, Georgia   John Carver
June 1997   Miriam Mayhew Carver

Acknowledgments

This book had its birth in our dealings with our many clients over the years—boards and CEOs leading organizations of many types in nonprofit, governmental, and business sectors, with many cultural backgrounds, and on three continents. It is to these leaders bold enough to pioneer a new vision of governance we owe our most hearty acknowledgments.

We must thank Jossey-Bass Publishers and our editor, Alan Shrader, for wise advice, occasional prodding, and good humor. Because our writing is forced to co-exist with our two respective very busy consulting schedules, we appreciate our executive assistant, Ivan Benson, who not only manages our consulting practices faithfully, but does so with a personable warmth that never seems even to have bad days.

—J. C. and M. M. C.

The Authors

John Carver, creator of the Policy Governance model of board leadership, is widely regarded not only as the most published but as the world's most provocative authority on governing boards. He has served as CEO and board member for various health organizations. He received his B.S. degree (1964) in business and economics and his M.Ed. degree (1965) in educational psychology from the University of Tennessee at Chattanooga. He received his Ph.D. degree (1968) in clinical psychology from Emory University, Atlanta. Carver has testified before the U.S. Congress, chaired the board of the National Council of Community Mental Health Centers, and consulted with clients on six continents. He has served as adjunct and visiting faculty with the University of Tennessee Space Institute, the University of Texas, Tulane University, and the University of Minnesota.

Miriam Mayhew Carver received most of her formal education in England, where she grew up. She received her B.A. degree (1973) from the University of East Anglia, Norwich. After moving to Canada in 1975, she completed her master's degree at Wilfrid Laurier University in Waterloo, Ontario. She has held a number of management positions in health and social service organizations. Her CEO experience was gained first as executive director of Canada's first AIDS hospice and then as executive director of a provincial association of counseling agencies. She has consulted in North America and in England with the boards of numerous organizations including health, education, social service, charity, association, mental health, and library organizations, as well as city councils.

John and Miriam Carver reside and base their consulting practices in Atlanta. They have previously coauthored one book, as well as three installments in the Jossey-Bass CarverGuide series.

Reinventing Your Board

Preparing for Change

Part One deals with the various factors a board must consider in setting out on its change process. We discuss the preparations that will help a board to implement Policy Governance successfully, and we answer some commonly asked questions. A brief theoretical overview of Policy Governance is presented along with our hints about the ways in which conceptual errors may hinder your board's implementation.

PART FOUR

Preparing for Change

| **Setting the Stage**

This is great in theory, but how do you actually do it?

In teaching the principles of the Policy Governance model to boards all over North America (and beyond), we have become accustomed to hearing some typical questions. The one that opens this chapter is among the most common. People are generally drawn to the simple logic of Policy Governance, but they recognize that it differs radically from their experience of boards and the board-staff relationship. Indeed, how *do* you actually do it?

It's a good question. Policy Governance, like any important job, is a process that has to be done right. The board is at the top of any organization, with authority over and accountability for that organization. With that kind of leverage, getting governance wrong is costly.

Implementing the Policy Governance model means developing your governing policies according to the principles of the model, then consistently using these unique documents according to those same principles. The largest part of this book (Part Two) will guide you through a process of developing those policies. But first, how can your board get ready to embark on the process of creating policies?

In order to implement Policy Governance, your board members must understand its theoretical principles. We hope that all board members are already familiar with the model. Still, it will be helpful to refer frequently to *Boards That Make a Difference* or to our theoretical review in Chapter Two of this book.

This chapter helps you set the stage for a successful change process. What follows are some frequently asked questions about the process of developing policies. They give us the opportunity to suggest methods and procedures that you may find useful in planning your work.

Are there situations or organizations in which Policy Governance is not appropriate?

Policy Governance was designed to be generic, so it should be applicable whenever a board faces the task of governing. The fundamental model does not require that an organization have a CEO, or even a staff, in order for the model to work (though these extensions of board authority make Policy Governance work better). The model does not depend on the organization's being a start-up operation or a mature one. And it is not related to whether an organization is for-profit, nonprofit, or governmental. We have certainly found situations in which Policy Governance is more difficult to implement. We have found that varying types of organizations and circumstances impose idiosyncrasies on the way the model is applied. But our interactions with board members and executives in widely different cultures from several continents support our confident assertion that the model works well in any situation.

Since Policy Governance creates a powerful board, why would it be attractive to CEOs?

Policy Governance does, indeed, strengthen the governing role, but it does not undercut legitimate CEO prerogatives. For most CEOs in public and nonprofit organizations, executive authority will be greater under Policy Governance than under traditional governance. To be more accurate, however, whether the CEO is more powerful or not is a function of how the board has been operating prior to Policy Governance. If the board has been rubber stamping everything the CEO wants done, then perhaps the CEO loses some power. If the board has been intruding into management, then the CEO gains some power. But Policy Governance is not about the board controlling more or less. It is about the board controlling the right things appropriately. So what can always be counted on under Policy Governance is that board and CEO prerogatives are far clearer and more rationally derived. Since the greatest source of stress for most CEOs is board behavior (as distinct from the straightforward pressure to perform), Policy Governance offers a more sane, even if more demanding, work environment.

How do we run two concurrent governance systems while moving toward Policy Governance?

You don't. You continue to govern as you always did until you are ready to use Policy Governance. Your board will be aware as it develops its policies that its new governance will result in the abandonment of much of the old system, and the sense of living in two worlds may well be bewildering. So rapid development of the new governance will minimize the confusion of having two approaches side by side. We caution you however not to change what you are doing until you are ready to change it *all*. Incremental governance change does not require this all-or-nothing care, but paradigm shifts—like the move to Policy Governance—are best made in this way. So once you have started the process of policy development, try to complete it as soon as you can.

Where do we begin, with policies about where we want to go (ends) or with policies about who does what to get there (means)?

We strongly recommend that your board develop all its policies restricting the means choices of the CEO (Executive Limitations) and those describing its own means (Governance Process and Board-CEO Linkage) before proceeding to Ends policies. You may find it odd to develop policies about means before determining Ends. We recommend this sequence because it enables the board to be clear about its own job and the jobs of its officers and committees, as well as to clarify the authority of the CEO early in the process. We have observed that boards traditionally fail to attend to Ends issues largely because they are so distracted by immediate means concerns. Further, completing means policies first allows the model to be adopted and put into use even before the board gives its full (and invariably more time-consuming) attention to Ends issues. When the board gets to Ends, it begins a job that remains its ongoing focus in perpetuity.

If it still seems illogical to make policy about staff means before having made policy about Ends, remember that in Policy Governance the board does not enact staff means policies that instruct the CEO how to do his or her job. Instead it enacts policies that prohibit some board-determined unacceptable means.

Just so we don't confuse you, we occasionally refer to Governance Process and Board-CEO Linkage categories, taken together, as *board means*—as distinguished from *staff means*. Staff means, of course, are board-controlled by the use of Executive Limitations policies. We employ another convention as well: we use lowercase when we speak of "ends" as a concept or idea, but we capitalize the word when referring to the policy category, Ends.

Which means policies should be developed first?

Part Two of this book includes a chapter for each of the policy categories used in Policy Governance. As to policies that deal with staff means and board means (omitting Ends for a moment), we have arranged them with the chapter on Executive Limitations policies first, then the chapter on Governance Process policies, followed by Board-CEO Linkage policies. There would be no problem with following exactly this order as your board proceeds through its policy development work. On the other hand, your board may wish to use a different sequence. Since none of the policies will come into effect until all three categories are completed, it really does not matter which of these three categories is completed first. Your board may have its own preference.

Many boards prefer to start with Executive Limitations, since these cover the issues that boards are ordinarily most worried about. There is some logic to this. When things go embarrassingly wrong in organizations, staff means issues are usually involved. Your board may wish to establish these controls on the CEO early. But some boards elect not to work first on Executive Limitations—the only negatively worded policies—for they prefer not to start on a negative note.

A number of boards we've worked with prefer to deal with Governance Process policies first, since they clarify the job of the board. Like them, your board may wish to start by establishing the expectations that it will have of itself before moving on to instructions to the CEO.

Still other boards begin by examining carefully the concept of CEO as it is used in Policy Governance. These boards start their policy development in the Board-CEO Linkage section. If this is your board's choice, remember that it will have to leave one of the Board-CEO Linkage policies incomplete (the Monitoring Policy) until Executive Limitations policies have been completed. That is because the Monitoring Policy sets forth the frequency and method of monitoring Executive Limitations and Ends policies, neither of which would have been created at this time.

Should we start from a blank sheet of paper?

Except for your work with Ends (which must begin from scratch), we wouldn't recommend it. You will find yourselves engaged in the deadly art of group writing before you know it! In fact, a major use of this book is to provide model policies that can be points of departure in developing your own policies. The policies that you will find in this book may not say what you need to say. They may exclude values that you strongly need to include in your policies. But they are a model-consistent starting point. We suggest that when your board works on the policies that make the Policy Governance model a reality for your board, you work systematically through the examples we have offered, changing them to reflect the values that your board wants to express. You must follow the principles about policy *format,* which we discuss in the next chapter, but the *content* of the policies is for you to make value judgments about.

Should we hire a consultant to help?

Arguments can be made in support of either using or not using such help. First, a consultant is *not* a help if he or she does not know the Policy Governance model *thoroughly.* Since Policy Governance has achieved a measure of popularity, many consultants have begun professing expertise that they do not have. We recommend that you inquire carefully into where they received their training in the model's theory and implementation. Second, a trained consultant is going to add to the up-front cost of the change process your board will go through. If the consultant is fully qualified, this help will almost certainly be worth the cost. However, a board that can take itself quickly through policy development may not need additional help. If there is a risk that your board will take months to develop its policies, it will be worth the cost to hire a consultant, for a properly trained person can guide most boards through most policies in one or two long days of hard work. The larger the organization, the more the cost of consulting help is cheap insurance against faltering in the process of implementation. In any event, this book is designed for use with and without consulting help.

If we don't use a consultant, should the chair lead the process?

Anyone on the board who knows the model well can lead the process. Sometimes the chair is the person most familiar and comfortable with the model, but if this is not true for your board, don't use the chair as the leader of the process. It *is* useful to have a designated leader in the work of developing governing policies, but who that person is may not be important. Choose someone who knows the model well, who can help the board stay on track, and who can include everyone in value discussions. Then, having chosen your workshop leader, let that person lead.

Can the CEO be the leader?

Great care should be taken to keep the CEO's role separate from the role of the board. The board can delegate a great deal to the CEO, but to avoid role confusion, it should not give the CEO responsibility for any part of the board's governance. Still, if the person with the best knowledge of the Policy Governance model is the CEO, it may seem wasteful not to use the CEO's expertise. If you decide to use the CEO as your leader, arrive with him or her at an understanding that the role to be performed is one of facilitation *only*. The CEO should not influence governance decisions beyond making relevant information available.

Should the CEO be present during the board's policy development work?

Yes. The CEO is a valuable resource. He or she has a great deal of information that the board may need in developing its policies. Not to use one of the board's most valuable resources would be a shame. The CEO, however, should not be making, but simply informing, board decisions.

Should other staff be present during the board's policy development work?

The other staff work for the CEO. Let the CEO decide. He or she will probably need the voices of other staff from time to time to contribute information that is relevant to the board's discussion. As you will see shortly, there will also be a need for someone to take careful notes.

Shouldn't a staff member keep a record of the board's policy development?

As your board makes its decisions about policy content, make sure someone writes them down. After the work, a copy of the board's own version of policies can be prepared from the discussion. The person who writes down the board's decisions can be anyone on the board or the CEO. If the board chooses the CEO, the CEO can bring in a staff member to carry out his or her responsibility.

What happens to our current distinction between policy and procedure?

You no longer need it. It is a distinction left over from having no technology of governance and, in light of that, doing whatever we could to find some way to differentiate board work and staff work. A framework designed specifically for the board's job changes all that. With Policy Governance, the distinctions are only (1) type of decision or policy—the four categories we discuss in detail in Chapter Three—and (2) size of decision or policy. These are the *only* distinctions, and they make unnecessary any further worry about policy versus procedure, strategy versus tactics, policy versus administration, or goals versus objectives. To drag these old distinctions over into your Policy Governance practice will reduce your effectiveness.

We already have a number of policies. Will that give us a head start?

Unfortunately, in all likelihood it will not, except perhaps in a minor way. Develop your new Policy Governance policies as if you have never had policies or made decisions at all. We know that advice will sound wasteful of your time, but we can assure you that it, in fact, saves a great deal of time. Previous decision making by the board, in policy form or not, will have been undertaken in traditional ways. That means Policy Governance policy categories would not have been used, staff means would have been prescribed, the integrity of policy levels would not have been observed, and the CEO role may not have been construed appropriately. So by starting the policy development process from scratch, you can avoid having to untangle all those complicators.

Only after you have completed your Policy Governance policy development should you refer to previous policies or decisions. At this point your new work provides you a model-consistent framework to which you can add or alter features. A previous investment policy, for example, may have resulted from careful and intelligent thinking about the safety of monetary instruments. Although the old policy may not have been worded in a way consistent with Policy Governance principles, the core intelligence in the previous work can be abstracted and applied to new asset protection policy.

Should we do a little work at each board meeting, or should we hold a retreat?

We know boards that have decided to develop their policies during regular board meetings, putting aside perhaps an hour from the regular agenda to work on a few policies at a time. This may work for your board, but the approach has a number of drawbacks. First, its use means that implementing the Policy Gover-

nance model *must* take several months, during which the board
and the CEO must deal with the confusion of having two very different governance systems in their consciousness. Second, a traditional agenda that tends to focus on the emergent rather than the
important can overwhelm a more conceptual approach, and it is
not uncommon to see that the items put off until next time are the
policy items. Consequently, we always recommend that the board
set aside a day or two for an intensive policy development retreat.

How long should the retreat be?

We have found that organizations not subject to great external
regulation can complete their board and staff means policies in a
day or two, if they use a competent consultant. City councils and
school boards, because of the highly regulated circumstances in
which they operate, take longer to do their work, and we expect
three days to be a minimum time for board and staff means policy
development to be accomplished. Without using a consultant, it is
likely that all board and staff means policies will not be completed
in the time even a long retreat can provide. Therefore, more than
one retreat will be needed.

As important as the length of time is the presence of all board
members during deliberations. The change being wrought in governance is so massive that board members not involved will face
culture shock upon returning. We normally ask boards to secure a
prior agreement from nonattending members to accept the policies
developed by those who attend (unless they have ethical reserva-
tions about them). Otherwise, nonattenders exercise dispropor-
tionate control over whether the board moves ahead.

*We have not made a final decision to use Policy Governance. How does this
affect policy development?*

We commonly work with boards in your position. The board is
not yet ready to commit to using the model, but it goes through
policy development as a way of finding out, What would it look like
for us? For many boards, this is a strategy that makes sense, for
drafting the policies provides a more concrete understanding of
the model.

We would recommend that even if the board has not made a final decision, it should develop its policies *as if it were definitely going to rely on them.* Policies in Policy Governance, unlike in traditional governance, constitute *all* the board has to say. It is important to develop policies from the perspective that there is no second, back-up document somewhere. This thorough reliance on policies demands a more complete and more rigorously prepared policy product. Boards that develop policies as a mere exercise rather than for actual use will not enhance their ability to make an informed choice between Policy Governance and what they are already doing. If they were to subsequently decide for Policy Governance, the tentatively drafted policies would have to be deliberated all over again. What an unnecessary duplication of effort!

We have made a decision to use Policy Governance, but a few of our members voted against this decision and are unhappy with it. What should we do?

Deciding to radically alter a board's governance system is a big step. It is not surprising that some people do not agree that it is a necessary or desirable step. Assuming that all the board members present at the meeting when the decision was made to use Policy Governance had an opportunity to voice their points of view, then the decision *is the board's decision.* Good governance makes a distinction between the position of the board and the minority position of a dissenter or dissenters. It calls upon boards to expect their members to adhere to board decisions until they are changed by the board. It explicitly vetoes the use or attempted use of personal power over the organization by individual members of the board. In other words, in *any* matter, not just that of the governance system to be used, the board members who voted against the board's final position are duty bound to respect that position, that is, not to undermine or sabotage it. If they cannot do this, they should consider resigning from the board. The worst outcome is that a nonunanimous vote leads to a half-hearted pursuit of the decision. You may have voted 6–3 to use Policy Governance, but if it is to be successful, you must pursue it with the resolve of 9–0.

Wouldn't using one model alone be like putting all our eggs in one basket?

No. These are not analogous situations. Consistently using one model is like having all the little wheels and other components in your wristwatch make sense as a total system. There would be no value in your purchasing a few extra wheels not designed for that specific watch just to be on the safe side. It is the system-specific, uncluttered integration of parts that makes the watch work. Admittedly, the parts must actually work as a system, but even if they do not, the solution is not to throw more parts at the watch but to redesign the system.

We could save so much time by just borrowing a similar organization's policies!

You could save time just as you could save a trip to the doctor by borrowing a friend's diagnosis! Board policies in Policy Governance are the board's soul. They do not contain all the values board members hold, but they do contain all the values that (1) the board as a whole can agree it holds and (2) all those necessary for proper governance of the organization. Not only does the policy *product* represent a compendium very personal to a specific board, but the *process* by which the policies are developed is itself at the heart of board leadership. If you install some other board's policies, or if you have your staff write the policies so you can adopt them, expect Policy Governance not to work for you.

Let us give you a small proviso. If the other organization's policies are well constructed, you may be able to use them as we use policy samples in Part Two of this book. But to make this work, you have to go through all the steps of inquiry and soul searching that your friendly benefactor board went through. To get Policy Governance off the ground, there is no free launch.

Policy Governance relies a lot on the CEO or board chair making "reasonable interpretations." Isn't this a lax and perhaps even risky leap of faith?

Actually, boards have no choice but to allow their delegates to interpret their words. There are thousands of decisions going on in any organization daily, all of which trace their origin back to more global board decisions. Policy Governance simply recognizes this unavoidable phenomenon and formulates a system in which the risk in interpretations is *reduced*. A board must be careful about the words it uses, just as any craftsperson is careful with his or her tools. Given that the board assumes responsibility for its words, the board chair and CEO in their respective domains can now move on as decision makers with confidence, knowing the board only expects reasonableness.

Naturally, if the board professes to give its delegatees the right of reasonable interpretation, it must actually do so or risk the loss of trust by delegatees. For example, if the board holds the CEO accountable for what the board wishes it had said or what it had in mind instead of what it actually said, then the board will have reneged on its agreement to accept *any interpretation that is reasonable*. Or if the board allows one board member's opinion (such as that of a treasurer or other expert) to be the only "reasonable interpretation" allowed, then it has similarly broken its agreement.

We have seen many instances of boards failing to implement Policy Governance well due to one hurdle or another. We have never yet found the rule about any reasonable interpretation to be a significant stumbling block. The rule contributes the same utility that the "reasonable person test" has made possible in law for generations.

Next Chapter

In Chapter Two, we review Policy Governance as a theory of board leadership. As we have pointed out, this book is not intended to be a theoretical text but rather a guide to practice. Consequently, our treatment of the fundamental principles of Policy Governance in the next chapter is brief.

Chapter Two

The Theoretical Foundation

Policy Governance offers not a mere improvement in board leadership but a revolution in board room behavior and in the governance-management relationship. It cannot be implemented by changing language (for example, by mistakenly calling goals *Ends*) or by making a few adjustments. If your board wishes to use this more sophisticated model of governance, you must not only understand the theory but be prepared for major changes in actual behavior and appearances.

This book is not intended to convey the theory in detail. If it were, it would be a rewrite of *Boards That Make a Difference*. Rather, this book is meant to aid persons who should already be acquainted with the concepts to (1) deal with the specifics of implementation and in doing so (2) acquire a deeper understanding of the theory. In this chapter, however, we briefly review the theory. Subsequent chapters are devoted to the practical aspects of implementation, though we occasionally return to theory throughout the book when doing so will aid understanding. Perhaps this reflects our agreement with Edwards Deming and John Milton, who claimed, respectively, that, "There is nothing so practical as a good theory" and "A good principle, not rightly understood, may prove as harmful as a bad principle."

The Policy Governance model takes as its starting point the principle that a governing board is accountable for the organization it governs and that it exists on behalf of a larger group of persons who, either legally or morally, own the organization. Since nonprofit and public organizations do not have stockholders, for them the concept of *moral* ownership may be the most valuable. This principle in itself separates Policy Governance boards from those that see themselves, often by default, as existing in order to represent staff, consumers, or other stakeholder groups of less broad legitimacy than stockholders—or stockholder equivalents. The principle forces the board to consider and answer the questions, From whom do we obtain our authority? and, To whom are we accountable? This is no easy task but is a necessary one, and it demands that the board distinguish theoretically between owners and other stakeholders, particularly customers.

For most community organizations, the community as a whole owns the organization; for membership associations, the members are owners. Owners may be customers as well, of course, but these are separate roles that governing boards must learn to distinguish.

When the board has decided to whom it is accountable, it must then settle the question, For what are we accountable? While statutes can sometimes help to answer this question, Policy Governance suggests that a generic statement of any governing board's accountability is that it must, acting on behalf of an identifiable ownership, ensure that the organization achieves what it should while avoiding what is unacceptable. This formulation sets the stage for the type of policy development necessary to implement the Policy Governance model. It also strongly implies some characteristics of the board job. First, in order to ensure that expectations are met, they must initially be stated, then delegated, and then checked for compliance. Hence a board defines, delegates, and monitors but probably does not carry out organizational work. Second, the board must act as a body, or it will risk giving contradictory definitions of its expectations. Hence the corporate nature of the board—its "groupness"—is an essential element of its modus operandi.

The board of directors, then, answerable to its ownership, must as a body define its expectations, assign these expectations to someone, and check that they were met. It will normally have expectations of a number of parties:

- *Itself.* The board must enunciate the expectations it has of its own operation, its use of officers and committees, its knowledge base, its connectedness to the ownership, its manner of delegating to others, and its method of monitoring its delegatees.

- *Its CEO.* The CEO, by whatever formal title, reports to the board and is the recipient of all executive authority passed into the operating organization. This officer is held accountable by the board for organizational performance. The board must provide direction to its CEO in such a way as to preserve board accountability while maximizing CEO flexibility, creativity, and freedom.
- *Its chair.* The board must demand certain performance from its chair, as it will authorize its chair to make decisions on its behalf. The chair's authority to make decisions will be in an area separate from that given to the CEO.
- *Its committees.* From time to time a board may find it helpful to have certain tasks carried out by smaller groups, particularly the task of gathering information and seeking options. It is important that such committees or task forces work in the service of the board and spend only those resources that the board thinks the committees' products are worth.

A Policy Framework That Works

The policy framework in Policy Governance can be seen as a comprehensive, carefully crafted way for a board to clarify all its expectations and values. To do so requires the board to conceive of organizational issues as either ends or means and address both types of issues differentially. We are not concerned, by the way, that these clarifications be called *policies,* but we are concerned that they follow a certain highly effective discipline in their concept and format. You could define these policies simply as the *values or perspectives that underlie action.*

Organizational Issues: Ends

There are many definitions of *ends,* but only one captures the concept meant by Policy Governance. Ends policies describe the board's expectations about (1) the benefit, difference, or outcome in consumers' lives that the organization is to produce, (2) the persons for whom the difference is to be made, that is, the designation of the consumers, and (3) the cost or relative worth of the benefit. Note that the term *ends* is not synonymous with *results* but is a complex of three components, one of which is results—and results that must be consumer benefit results rather than a result of some other type (such as excellent staff morale).

Ends are therefore *not* defined as simply anything that seems important to someone, or anything someone on the board is interested in, or what someone thinks should be exclusively board work, or the end point in a process, although we have seen all of these mistaken definitions used. Ends simply answer the questions, What good? For which people? At what cost? Ends issues— particularly the components that describe results and the cost of results—are largely ignored by traditional boards, since the focus of typical boards is on staff methods and practices. Thus Policy Governance boards, by distinguishing ends from means, can give discrete, highly focused attention to the ends toward which all activities should be directed. Ends policies, because they describe and compel organizational achievement, are instructive to the CEO.

Organizational Issues: Means

The Policy Governance model defines *means* as any organizational issues that are not ends—an exclusion definition. The term is not simply synonymous with *methods,* though it includes methods along with practices, situations, circumstances, activities, and *any* organizational aspect that is not a *direct* definition of results, recipients of results, or the cost or relative worth of those results.

Thus the board's own job of governing, along with its procedures and practices, are board means issues. The board's policies about its own means are instructive, not to the CEO but to the board itself, its chair, and, if applicable, its committees. On the other hand, operational methods such as services, programs, finances, and personnel are staff means issues. Board policies about staff means are instructive to the CEO. Boards traditionally involve themselves deeply in staff means issues. Policy Governance boards, on the other hand, involve themselves in staff means only as far as needed to safely let go of them.

Since boards are ultimately accountable for both ends and means, they must be in control of both categories of issues. That is, they have not only the right but the obligation to govern both. Policy Governance allows boards to make policy controlling both types of issues, though preserving a dominant focus on ends. The ends focus is warranted, since it is ends that justify having an organization in the first place; explicit definition of ends defines organizational success. As to staff means, the model allows boards to control them responsibly, while minimizing board interference in the acceptable variation among approaches to staff work.

How does the model enable both control and flexibility? It tells the board to control ends and means through policy (rather than through review of or participation in distinct decisions) but to express policies that control ends and means in different ways. Ends policies should be prescriptive, that is expressed positively, as in the example, "The XYZ agency exists so that homeless teenagers will secure safe housing and job skills." Staff means policies, on the other hand, should be proscriptive, as in the example, "In pursuit of the Ends, the CEO may use any available means except that he or she may not allow this programmatic practice or that fiscal ratio." This approach demands that the board compile a "don't-do-it" list, a counterintuitive but effective technique that frees boards from the need to redo, review, rehash, or second guess staff work. The don't-do-it policies are called *Executive Limitations policies*. Boards as a result have time to attend to their own jobs and stay largely engaged in the study, consultation, and value-laden decision making required for Ends determination.

Delegation to the CEO is very powerful using such a system, for the CEO no longer has to guess about what ends are expected and which means are prohibited. The Policy Governance board tells its CEO that he or she is to achieve the ends required by the board within the constraints on means imposed by the board. Such a method of delegation does not depend on the CEO seeking board approvals, since anything true to the policies is, as it were, pre-approved.

It is obvious that if a board is to control and direct the organization through the establishment and monitoring of ends and means policies, then the policies it creates must be inclusive, complete, and comprehensive. It no longer suffices to have a policy about this and a policy about that, as the this's and thats happen to occur to board members and staff. You cannot govern by

policy as long as policies are merely a patchwork of pronouncements. How does the board ensure that its policies have no significant gaps? Regarding staff practices and situations, if the CEO can
use any means that the board has not prohibited, how can the
board be sure it has not forgotten something quite critical that
should have been put off-limits? These issues are answered in Policy Governance by conceiving of policies as occurring in cascading
levels. Policies do, after all, come in sizes.

Policies reflect statements of value, and values can be seen to
vary in size or breadth. Some values can be stated broadly, leaving
a wide range of interpretation. Others can be stated more narrowly,
leaving less to interpretation. Policy Governance asks boards to
view values as a nested set, with large values "cradling" smaller
ones. To control such a set, the board must first control the largest
member of the set. This is obvious with a physical nested set, such
as a set of mixing bowls, as shown in Figure 2.1.

Tighter control, or control of smaller values, is established by
expanding the direct (hands-on) control into the nested set, one
layer at a time. Control over the smaller values is indirect (hands-
off), but no less real, as shown in Figure 2.2.

Figure 2.1. A Nested Set.

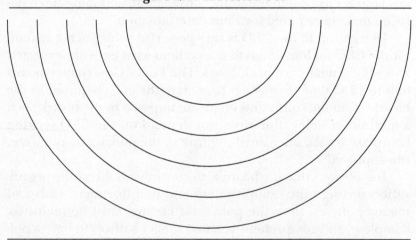

Note: Smaller bowls fit within larger bowls as smaller issues fit within larger
ones. The entire set of bowls can be controlled by handling only the outermost
bowl.

This method allows the board to establish overall or broad-level control, which is obligatory, and to establish further, more detailed control, which is optional. By taking control over successively smaller values, the board can proceed to increase its control in increments. The increments are added until the board has established a level of control that will enable it to allow a delegatee to use any reasonable interpretation within the decision range that remains. This is the point at which the board delegates.

A board may express an ends value very broadly. An example is, "Homeless teenagers will secure safe housing and job skills." This statement may be seen as the value represented by the "largest-mixing-bowl." The board could choose to conclude its direct control at this point but must be willing for the CEO to use any reasonable interpretation of this broad prescription as he or she manages the enterprise. It is more likely that the board will want to define these words further before turning the matter over to the CEO. If so, it may add, "Among homeless teenagers, minority or

Figure 2.2. Hands-On and Hands-Off Control.

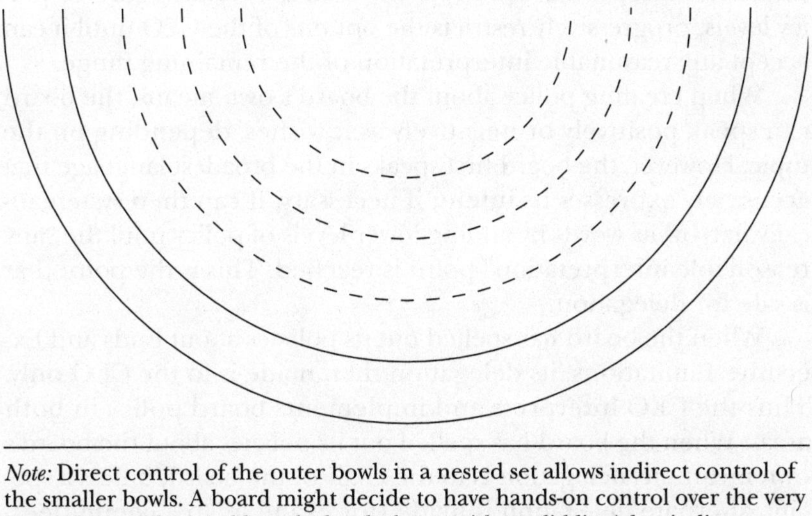

Note: Direct control of the outer bowls in a nested set allows indirect control of the smaller bowls. A board might decide to have hands-on control over the very largest issues (depicted here by bowls drawn with a solid line) but indirect or hands-off control of smaller issues (depicted by bowls drawn with a broken line).

handicapped persons will be given priority." This last statement constitutes the second-largest-mixing-bowl value.

Other clarifications would be considered at this second level. For example, the board may add that the job skills it intends homeless teenagers to receive are those that enable speedy, minimal self-sufficiency and that by "safe housing," it means that which provides freedom from harm or harassment. Again the board might stop here or, if it is unwilling to let the CEO choose any reasonable interpretation of its words in this second level, it may go further to define the words used in the second level of policy by creating a third level. And it can further define these words, too. The rule is simply that the board defines its words in increasing detail until it is able to allow the delegatee to use *any* reasonable interpretation.

The same procedure is followed when the board makes policy about means. Policy about staff means is created in the admittedly counterintuitive negative language explained earlier. Such policies are called *Executive Limitations policies,* in that they place limits on executive authority. The Level One, or largest and most inclusive proscriptive policy, is commonly worded something like this: "The CEO shall not cause or allow any decision, action, condition, or organizational circumstance that is illegal, imprudent, or contrary to commonly accepted business and professional ethics." Further definition of these words follows as the board, by adding further policy levels, progressively restricts the options of the CEO until it can accept any reasonable interpretation of the remaining range.

When creating policy about the board's own means, the board can speak positively or negatively as it wishes, depending on the topic. However, the board first speaks in the broadest language that accurately expresses its intent; if necessary, it can then systematically narrow its words by adding lower levels of policy until the "any reasonable interpretation" point is reached. This is the point that is safe for delegation.

When the board has spelled out its policies about Ends and Executive Limitations, its delegation then made is to the CEO only. Thus the CEO interprets and implements board policy in both areas. When the board has spelled out its policies about the board's own means, its delegation is to the chair of the board, unless a specific alternate delegation is made (for example, to a committee). Board means fall into two categories. First, Governance Process policies describe the board's definition of its job, as well as that of the chair and any committees it forms. Second, Board-CEO Linkage policies describe the manner of connecting governance and management, that is, how authority will be delegated and how the board will monitor performance.

Finding Your Way on the Policy Circle

We will use a circle diagram (Figure 2.3) to present the emerging policy material as we trace policy development in Part Two. We introduce it here because we have found the diagram useful in helping boards to stay clear about where they are in the process. Assume that the four categories of policies can be represented by four sets of mixing bowls like those previously described. Using two-dimensional bowls, of course, we can display these four sets so that like-sized bowls in the different sets meet. Remember, *all* organizational decisions, situations, activities, and production fit somewhere in these exhaustive categories. That is, the circle as drawn encloses all possible organizational issues—none are left out.

View the resulting set of concentric circles in this way: note that there are four quadrants, each including every possible decision within the topic of the respective categories. There are various levels represented, corresponding to the larger and smaller issues, decisions, or values within that category. The lines further inside the circle, away from the circumference, are smaller decisions, ones contained inside the larger decisions represented by those nearer to and on the circumference.

Figure 2.4 shows the same circle. In Figure 2.4, however, board decision making has reached different depths within each of the four quadrants. This diagram demonstrates what board policy making is really like under Policy Governance. There is always policy at the outside edge of the circle (largest-mixing-bowl level of policy), while inside each quadrant, policies will have been developed to various depths depending on board values. The deeper the area of board policy, the more detailed it is and the fewer decisions left to whomever is delegated authority to make the remaining, lesser decisions.

Notice that the board chair and the CEO are both empowered to interpret and implement board policy but that this power

Figure 2.3. The Policy Circle.

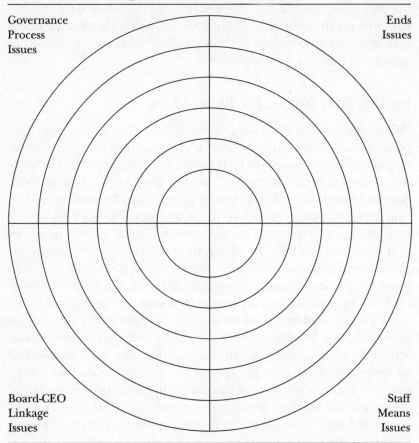

Governance Process Issues

Ends Issues

Board-CEO Linkage Issues

Staff Means Issues

Note: The four categories of organizational issues are shown as four sets of bowls, brought together to form four quadrants of a circle. Larger and smaller issues within those categories are shown as larger and smaller bowls. For easier reference throughout this book, differing categories and sizes of issues are brought together as series of concentric circles across four quadrants.

applies *in different domains*. The chair has no authority over staff functions (does not show up on the right side of the circle), and the CEO has no authority over the board's governance (does not show up on the left side of the circle). This arrangement corrects a traditional governance flaw wherein the chair is compelled to usurp board authority in dealing with the CEO (supervising, directing, making demands the board never made) while at the same

Figure 2.4. Board Policy Making.

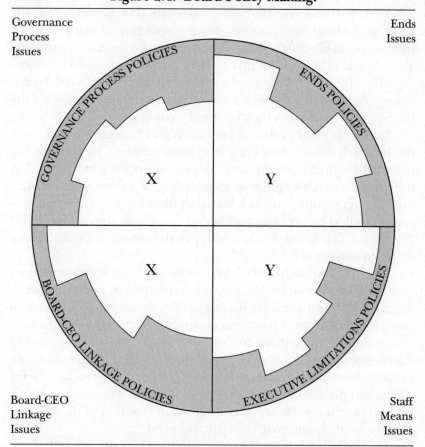

Governance
Process
Issues

Ends
Issues

Board-CEO
Linkage
Issues

Staff
Means
Issues

Note: Completed board policies will occupy the outer part of each quadrant but will come into more detail (smaller-bowl levels), the amount depending on the board's values. The board will go into more detail about some policy topics than others, even within a given quadrant. Notice that the quadrant containing all staff means issues will be addressed by the board in a constraining or negative fashion, hence the policy category titled *Executive Limitations*. Empty space in the middle represents smaller decisions the board is content to leave to delegatees. The board chair will be given authority to make decisions in spaces marked *X.* The CEO will be given authority to make decisions in spaces marked *Y.*

time *becoming* the de facto CEO (making decisions about organizational matters). Similarly, the opposite flaw is corrected; the CEO, while held fully accountable for operational matters, is not held accountable for the board's governance, agendas, orientation, attendance, or any of the myriad other aspects of board functioning with which CEOs have been inappropriately burdened. In this latter role, CEOs have typically assumed more responsibility for the board's acting responsibly than their boards have.

Notice also that in the areas of Ends and Executive Limitations, the board decides policies at a level appropriate to its concern but not further: thus it would never decide or approve an entire document such as a budget, a program plan, or a personnel manual. Such an act would place the board in direct control of smaller issues as well as larger ones and would needlessly remove flexibility from the CEO. Indeed, it would make definition of the CEO role all but meaningless.

Instead, the board would contemplate just what aspects or characteristics about budgeting, programming, or personnel management it would consider unacceptable. Reaching agreement on these matters, if the agreement is committed to paper, yields written guidelines to be given to the CEO. Thus, instead of approving a staff document, a process that invites board members into unending details, the board will have produced its own far briefer document disclosing what would lead to its *dis*approving staff documents or actions. Hence, anything *not* in violation of those board requirements is automatically preapproved.

This board task is both easy and hard. The easy part is that it is far briefer—the resulting board documents are quite short and simple—and it does not require board members to become expert in the topics being controlled. Accountants, for example, are no better at *governing* fiscal management than nonaccountants, even though they might be immeasurably better at fiscal *management*. The hard part is that this process takes more discipline. Self-restraint is called for if a board is to do the higher-level thinking required rather than jumping headlong into the more concrete, more familiar details of a topic—in spite of having a staff hired to deal with such matters.

The message for the CEO is an empowering one. "As long as our intended Ends are achieved and our Executive Limitations are not violated (and we'll be checking!), any plan you create or course you pursue is acceptable." The most vital test of means, of course, is not in the means themselves but in whether they produce the Ends. The board finds out if its Ends demands have been met, not by inspecting staff means but by monitoring the Ends policies. Traditional boards fool themselves into thinking they've monitored results by monitoring program activity.

Monitoring Compliance with Policies

The Policy Governance model holds that there can be no legitimate monitoring without pre-established criteria. Attempting to evaluate in the absence of criteria, while common, is both unfair and futile. Approval or acceptance of financial statements, budgets, or other plans are examples of what passes for monitoring but which, upon inspection, prove to be only ad hoc opinions expressed apropos of no criteria. These familiar practices are not monitoring at all—they are merely wandering around in the presence of data.

A Policy Governance board establishes its expectations about organizational performance by formulating Ends and Executive Limitations policies. Since these are the only board expectations, the provisions of these policies *are* the criteria it will then use to measure whether expectations have been met. Next, the board assigns a method and frequency of monitoring to each of the policies in order to receive performance assurance as often as it desires. The method of monitoring establishes how the data will find their way to the board (they can come from the CEO, but that is not the only route). Thus conceived, ongoing monitoring of board expectations is exactly the same as CEO performance evaluation, except in a more realistic and continual form than what traditional boards have known. In Chapter Six, which deals with Board-CEO Linkage policies, we explore the important issue of monitoring.

Designing Governance Structure

Throughout this overview of the Policy Governance model, we have emphasized that the board (not its subparts such as committees or individual members) should make its requirements clear and then monitor to see that they are met. For the board to carry out these responsibilities as a body requires it to avoid some traditional structural traps or circumstances that will mitigate against its ability to speak as a body. Board members are likely to disagree over important issues, so speaking with one voice will not be achieved by unanimity. It is, however, a requirement that all board members support the legitimacy of a board decision, even if they voted against it.

Traditional governance provides a number of ways for a board to become ineffective at voicing its corporate will. Permitting or inviting board officers or committees to be responsible as individuals for aspects of organizational performance destroys the board's ability to demand accountability from the CEO. Officers, particularly treasurers and chairs, are commonly put in such a position.

Bylaws often charge the chair with "responsibility for the general supervision of the organization." Or the ostensible CEO is said to report to the board through the chair or be supervised by the chair. Any of these arrangements makes the chair the de facto CEO in authority, although rarely is the chair then held accountable in a way that corresponds to this power. Consequently, chairs often "dip" in and out of the CEO role, a most disconcerting behavior to the intended CEO and a sure sign of undisciplined governance.

The treasurer is frequently described as being "responsible for the books of accounts, deposits, and receipts" or other words that assign responsibility for fiscal propriety. Yet the board must surely hold its CEO accountable for these matters. So just who is accountable? To hold the CEO accountable for conditions that the treasurer has the authority to direct is both unfair and organizationally irresponsible. Again, this unclear delegation is a sure sign of undisciplined governance.

Often other board members, as individuals, attempt to exert authority in the organization. Boards rarely know the extent of such individual renegadism, since unless they witness it, they can only become aware of it through staff tattling. Board members who act in such a manner may be doing so out of a genuine desire to help or advise. Notwithstanding noble intentions, the result of interference by individual board members is that the staff use organizational resources to carry out individual demands. Board member interference is nothing less than an abuse of position.

Boards must protect their organizations from such waste and misdirection by assuring the CEO that, while being held accountable for fulfilling written board policies, he or she *never* is expected to please board members as individuals. Thus a responsible board as a body protects its staff from itself as individuals.

Board committees are any groups set up by the board, instructed by the board, or reporting to the board, no matter what they are called (for example, task forces are included) or for how long they are to exist (that is, whether they are ad hoc or not). A board that, having first defined its job, decides to use a committee to help in the accomplishment of its job, is using the committee mechanism legitimately. But committees can damage the board's ability to hold its CEO accountable, just as can chairs and treasurers. A board that puts together a group in order to instruct about, advise about, help in, or share in any part of the responsibility delegated to the CEO is not using the committee mechanism legitimately. It has set up a circumstance that renders the board unable to instruct as a body, delegate to a single point in the system, or hold that point accountable for performance according to board-stated expectations. Who is to be held accountable if a course of action advised by a committee doesn't work?

It is a rule of Policy Governance that board committees may exist only to assist in the board's own job and never to involve themselves in the jobs of staff. It is worth noting that advice is indistinguishable from instruction when it comes from a higher authority. Staff who want advice can ask for it from anyone, including from board members (as individuals) if the staff decide that such individuals are good sources of advice. The CEO can then be held accountable for staff decisions, since whether or not staff members ask for or follow advice is up to them. Advice, in other words, is always invited and never imposed. The Policy Governance rule about committees usually results in boards disbanding personnel, program, facility, finance, property, publications, public relations, and many other committees.

Defining the Board's Job

Any job can be conceived as a package of values-added; the governing board's job is not an exception. Summarizing those values-added yields a global purpose for governance. The board's job is to see to it, on behalf of the owners, that the organization produces what it should (described in Ends policies) while avoiding situations and conduct that should not occur (described in Executive Limitations policies). This seems a simple statement until we examine what is necessary to assure its fulfillment. In order to fulfill its job, the board must:

- Clearly articulate who the owners are and then consult with them with a view to the board's crafting relevant Ends policies for the organization; otherwise it will not truly be able to act "on behalf of the owners."
- Make its rules for itself clear, or sufficient group discipline will never be maintained.
- Unambiguously assign the right to interpret and implement board policies to those who will be held accountable for policy compliance, else the board will be so overcome with details of subordinate jobs that its own will be undoable.
- Insist upon systematic, believable monitoring data that address the expectations it has established, or it can never be assured that its careful words have led to an acceptable reality.

Policy Governance provides tools for fulfilling this role, which include separating ends from means and then separating staff means from board means. Also included are arranging issues by size and dealing with the large ones first, leaving the smaller ones to delegatees when the board can accept any reasonable interpretation. Monitoring only against policy criteria is another tool.

Using these tools to accomplish the leadership with which boards are charged, *any* governing board should set out to produce the following values-added, as distinguished from the products of its staff:

1. A high-integrity linkage with the owners, that is, one that is unbiased and complete.
2. Written governing policies (Ends, Executive Limitations, Governance Process, and Board-CEO Linkage) in a constantly updated, succinct form.
3. Assurance of organizational performance, which is treated as CEO performance when such an officer exists.

These crucial job products are the nondelegatable minimum for the governing board of any organization. They cannot be handed over to the staff as can all other outputs. Each, of course, can be further defined, but these three are the basic points of departure in describing what every governing board must produce. In practice, a given board may choose to add other job outputs, but beyond these, any additional contributions the board selects to put on its own plate are optional.

Remember the following key points of theory before you go further. If you are unable to explain these points to someone else, you may need to review Policy Governance theory more thoroughly:

1. The board stands in for those who morally own the organization.
2. The board speaks with one voice or not at all. The board will allow no officer, committee, or individual on the board to come between the board and its CEO.
3. The board directs the organization by addressing Ends and Executive Limitations policies to the CEO.
4. The board instructs no staff but the CEO.
5. Ends and means are distinguished from each other only according to whether an issue describes (1) what outcome or difference is to be produced, (2) for whom it is to be produced, and (3) the worth or cost of the outcome. An issue that describes one or more of these attributes is an ends issue. An issue that does not describe one or more of these attributes is a means issue. That a matter is important does not make it an ends issue. That the board wishes to control an issue does not make it an ends issue. That a matter is controlled by law or custom does not make it an ends issue.
6. The board controls ends issues positively—by prescribing certain ones.
7. The board controls staff means issues negatively—by prohibiting certain ones.
8. The board defines issues from the most general level of specificity to that more detailed level which will allow it to delegate any reasonable interpretation of its words.
9. The board may change the level of its policy making at any time.
10. The board monitors performance against its policy words.

Next Chapter

Chapter Three deals with the implications your board should be ready to face if you choose to use the Policy Governance model. You must be ready to look at your job in a radically new way and to use the new principles consistently. While the implementation will give new clarity to the board's job and will empower both board and staff, it will not be without its difficulties. Being prepared for the implications of this new approach will help your hard work produce results.

Chapter Three

Deciding to Implement Policy Governance

If your board has taken the time required to become acquainted with Policy Governance, it then is confronted with a decision. Will you elect to use the model to conduct future board business? Many implications are to be considered in making this decision. Should the model be adopted in its entirety? How much trouble is the transition going to be? Is it worth the trouble? What will change about the meetings themselves? How will the staff react? How will the board's publics react?

A Policy Governance board must be ready to question all of its previous assumptions and practices. Using a model means that decisions and activities inconsistent with the model are no longer practiced, no matter how comfortably familiar they might be. You cannot play both football *and* baseball at the same time. In this chapter, we explore the implications of deciding to implement Policy Governance. We also examine some of the anxieties created by such a decision, as well as their resolution.

Boards of directors have traditionally operated in a manner based on habit, attention to the present rather than to the future, and the process referred to in *Boards That Make a Difference* as the *approval syndrome.* All of these approaches have a face validity accorded by tradition. But if your board wishes to govern by focusing primarily on results, recipients, and costs of results (ends) and by controlling unacceptable means, you must realize that your methods and meetings will change beyond recognition as a result. You must realize that the matters you will deliberate will change

33

substantially. You must realize that ritual actions and time-honored traditions will no longer substitute for real leadership. The process you are undertaking calls upon you to be disciplined as a group. Group discipline renders unacceptable many of the structures and activities we have all learned to believe are indispensable parts of governance.

Consequently, the decision to use this powerful and radically different approach to the board's job is a very major decision, one not to be taken lightly. Half using a powerful tool can be dangerous. Compromising between A and B can result in a product that is worse than either A or B, and may be a mess. We offer here, therefore, a series of issues to be considered by a board in its all-important deliberation on whether to revamp its governance style.

Partial or Total Implementation

We are often asked if it is necessary to accept the whole model, or if partial implementation is possible. Certainly, some principles of Policy Governance are useful in or out of the model. As an example, consider the principle that there can be no real monitoring of performance in the absence of preset criteria. This principle is one of basic fairness and has its place in any human endeavor when authority is held by one party over another. The concept of ownership is another part of Policy Governance that can be safely imported into another approach. Other parts of Policy Governance, however, cannot be used safely outside of the model. As an example, imagine the havoc that could result from a board's resolution to stop dictating staff practices (by approving staff recommendations or by even more meddlesome intrusions) when it has not first set up adequate controls to prevent unacceptable practices from occurring.

A model is by its very nature general. Any board seeking to use a model must tailor it to its particular circumstances. Tailoring, however is not the same as disassembling the model. Conceptual sloppiness easily sails under the otherwise respectable flag of tailoring. A model, in order to be useful and flexible among a variety of different organizations, must be built upon principles that fit together to form an internally consistent unit that makes sense as a whole. We understand that boards are reluctant to accept wholesale a model that so tests their ability to act consistently in their governing role. But we are unapologetic about our position that a board should first learn the model, then decide if it may be useful, and then if a decision to implement is made, should implement it rigorously in order to benefit from its powerful potential.

So your board should:

- Learn the principles of the model and decide if they make sense.
- Decide whether or not to use them.
- Try and find any reason that could justify *not* using principles that make sense.
- Use the principles to design the board's job in a way that fits the organization, yet still maintains conceptual integrity.

The Policy Categories

Common wisdom has long advocated that governing boards do their work through policy. Until Policy Governance, however, the subject of board policy has had little substance. Policy was whatever a board wanted to say it was, or policy was managerial matters raised to the board table. Policy Governance makes much of policy, but policy as a carefully crafted instrument for leaders leading leaders.

Policy Governance cannot be operationalized without at least three categories of organizational decisions for which the board is accountable and must address. The categories are *ends,* the *means of the staff,* and the *means of the board.* Because staff means are controlled by limiting rather than prescribing, we use Executive Limitations as the category title of board policies that address that area. In practice the category of board means is subdivided into two—Governance Process and Board-CEO Linkage. Therefore, despite there being three basic conceptual divisions, we refer to four categories of board policies: Ends, Executive Limitations, Governance Process, and Board-CEO Linkage. Failing to observe the strict definitions of these categories depowers the model. Our observation is that if a board fails to observe the different categories, the failure most often lies in obscuring the fundamental ends-means distinction.

Ends statements are simply and only those statements describing the good (or change or difference, or benefit or result) to be achieved by the organization, the recipients of that good, and the cost or worth of the good. Any statement that describes one or all of the three components is an ends statement. Any statement that does not describe at least one of these is not, no matter how important what is described is perceived to be. Hence, a reading program is not an ends issue, though literacy is. No services or programs are ends issues. Budgets are not ends issues, as they do not address the cost of the benefit but rather the component means costs of staff activity. Even fiscal soundness is not an ends issue. In fact, no statement that describes the activities or beliefs of the organization can be an ends statement; they are always means. Board members must remember that their opportunity to control staff means lies not in erroneously labeling them *ends* but in proscribing them in Executive Limitations policies.

If your board has decided to use Policy Governance, it should:

- Use the policy categories of Policy Governance, not those of management.
- Be rigorous about determining the policy category in which an issue belongs.
- Determine whether an issue is an ends, staff means, or board means issue before attempting to deal with it.

Not Everything Is a Board Issue

In one sense everything *is* a board issue, since the board is accountable for everything that goes on in the organization. But a system that responsibly distinguishes between the job of the board and that of the staff must delineate some issues that the board should not directly address even though accountable for them. Thus, when confronted with any issue from any source, boards must first decide which kind of issue it is. Boards must also decide what size issue it is, since boards will address the largest issue in any category, further defining until any reasonable interpretation by a delegatee would be acceptable.

Even if an issue is found to be an ends issue, the board should not assume it is a board issue before examining its size. A board using Policy Governance may have delegated issues of this size to the CEO, having already prescribed larger ends issues in the Ends policies. The board may always change its policies or take up issues of smaller magnitude, but in the absence of a decision to do so, any ends issue already delegated to the CEO would not even be discussed by the board.

If an issue is found to be a staff means issue, the board can only address it negatively and even then must first examine its size. Starting at the broadest level, the board will already have *proscribed* certain staff means in Executive Limitations policies and delegated the right to reasonably interpret these policies to the CEO. In the absence of a decision to change these policies, a matter in the delegated area, no matter how important or interesting, would not be decided or discussed by the board.

If an issue is found to be a board means issue, the board must first examine its size before admitting it to discussion. The board will have established policies that govern its own process starting at a broad, inclusive level and proceeding to further definition until delegation is made to the chair. The board should resist dealing with matters it has already delegated to the chair.

This discipline requires that the board, instead of discussing and deciding any issue that is raised, involve itself only in those issues that rightly belong to the board. We have found that this requirement sorely tests the resolve of boards that have previously acted as if any issue a board member wants to bring up is thereby a board issue, previously delegated or not. Implementing Policy Governance requires that this discipline be strictly observed.

If your board has decided to use Policy Governance, it should:

- Recognize that not all issues are board issues.
- Be rigorous about determining the size of issue being considered for discussion.
- Decide if an issue belongs to the board before debating it.

Those Negative Policies

Even when board members understand the theoretical reasons, it is common in implementation for boards to question the principle that staff means be controlled by the board through the use of negatively worded or proscriptive policies. A frequently voiced concern is that the language ("The CEO shall not cause or allow . . .") is awkward and is unacceptably negative in tone. While we are sympathetic to the complaint of awkwardness, we urge boards to notice that while proscriptive policies are verbally negative, they are psychologically very positive to the recipient. The message received is, "So long as you do not do these few proscribed things, *anything else* will have our support." This is the same as the board's pre-approving any action of the CEO that is not in violation of the board's pre-stated criteria about unacceptable means.

There is always some awkwardness when the board goes out of its way to keep from becoming involved in staff means. The difficulty is worth the trouble, because it makes possible a succinct way for the board to deal with its accountability for staff means. More time is therefore made available for the board's attention to Ends.

If your board has decided to use Policy Governance, it should:

- Understand that telling the CEO how to manage would be a never-ending process.
- Understand that if the board tells the CEO how to operate, it can no longer hold the CEO accountable for the results.
- Understand that constraining language allows greater empowerment.
- Get used to the awkwardness; it's worth it.

Board Control and Accountability

Without doubt, the board is accountable for everything that goes on in the organization. But the board cannot do, or even supervise, everything that goes on. Being accountable for something does not, therefore, answer the question of who is to do it. Accountability can be discharged by simply *seeing to it* that something is done. "Seeing to it" is achieved through (1) describing the "it" that is to be done, that is, describing success, (2) unambiguously assigning the "it" to someone, and (3) checking to be sure the "it" was done. In Policy Governance, the describing phase is expressed through the careful crafting of policies about what is to be achieved (Ends policies) and what is to be avoided (Executive Limitations policies). The assigning phase is accomplished by carefully defining a CEO role whenever the circumstances of the organization will allow it (Board-CEO Linkage policies). The checking phase consists of systematic monitoring (established in the Board-CEO Linkage policies) of organizational performance against the provisions of the Ends and Executive Limitations policies.

We are occasionally asked how we manage to talk boards into giving up control. We don't. On the contrary, we present a governance system that allows boards to be more in control *of the right things*. We point out that a board attending to whatever comes up cannot be sure that all the right things come up. Such a board is always behind the eight ball. Policy Governance puts the board in the front position and has it state from the broadest level to more defined levels what it expects from the organization and the CEO. In a similar vein, we have heard Policy Governance referred to as a "hands-off" model. This is not strictly true. In any organization there is too much going on for the board to have its hands on everything. Its challenge is to know what to have its hands on and what it can leave to its delegatee. Thus we would describe Policy Governance as a "hands off some things and hands on some things" model.

If your board has decided to use Policy Governance, it should:

- Realize that traditional governance provides the illusion that the board is in control.
- Understand that real control is its legal and moral obligation.
- Differentiate between the accountability for something happening and the job of doing it.
- Control the organization by broad, carefully categorized policies.

The Issue of Trust

Boards of directors often struggle with the issue of trust. They want to trust their staff, but they know that they are accountable for what the staff does. Policy Governance tells boards that trust is of less importance than (1) clarifying expectations and (2) monitoring them. Indeed, when boards complain that they do not trust their CEO, it is almost never clear what they do not trust the CEO to do or achieve. Trust problems virtually always stem from a board's not being clear about what it wants and doesn't want. If a board establishes Ends and Executive Limitations policies, it can gather monitoring data that disclose whether the CEO fulfilled a reasonable interpretation of their provisions. Following these steps renders trust of far less importance. The board's assurance that the organization is performing is now based on data, not trust. Ironically, under these conditions, confidence and faith flourish!

Frankly, the biggest trust issue between a board and its CEO is the CEO's ability to trust the board. Governing bodies that do not make their requirements known or that act without regard for how they said they would act are unpredictable and untrustworthy employers. CEOs and staffs find ways to protect themselves against board caprice, but such protection is rarely in the interest of organizational effectiveness. It is in the board's interest to arrange its governance so that the CEO can trust that treatment by the board will be fair and predictable.

If your board has decided to use Policy Governance, it should:

- Clearly state what its requirements of the CEO are.
- Be clear about what the CEO can expect from the board.
- Keep its word.

The Board's Use of the CEO

The term *CEO*—as we use it here—is not a title but a function. By whatever title used in a particular organization, the person granted the CEO role reports directly to the board and is held accountable for all organizational performance. The incumbent of this position must have the authority that allows this accountability to be realistic. Nonprofit and public organizations rarely have senior staff positions whose authority and accountability actually match this description. Often the most senior staff person (called, among other titles, executive director, president, general manager, superintendent, city manager) is held accountable for that which no corresponding authority has been delegated. Sometimes the authority has been delegated by the board in an overlapping way, for example to the ostensible CEO *and* to one or more board committees.

While boards rarely disagree that the single link between them and the operating organization should be the CEO, it is common to find that they have some tendency to instruct persons who report to the CEO. Boards using Policy Governance treat all staff accomplishments and failings, as measured against policies, as the accomplishments and failings of the CEO. This does not mean, of course, that boards should never talk to staff, but it does mean that they should neither instruct nor monitor the performance of persons in sub-CEO positions. Boards can usefully interact with sub-CEO staff about *board decisions,* particularly about Ends. They should not interact with staff about issues that have already been delegated to the CEO. In other words, it is permissible for a board to invite staff into its business but not permissible to invite itself into staff business.

If your board has decided to use Policy Governance, it should:

- Instruct only the CEO.
- View all organizational performance as that of the CEO.
- View any organizational failure to comply with board policy as the failure of the CEO.
- Require that the CEO keep the organizational performance within policy criteria and restore it to this state should there be policy violations.
- Never, in its official capacity, help the CEO manage.

Organizations with No CEO or Staff

The CEO in Policy Governance is a person held accountable by the board for achieving the Ends of the organization while avoiding the unacceptable means. Even very small organizations can use such a position. Boards that do not have a CEO have to deal with internal divisions of labor and the managing of the various parts of the organization themselves. This makes the board job harder than it would be with a CEO at the helm. Nonetheless, without a CEO, the principles of Policy Governance can still be helpful.

When there is no staff, the board is the workforce as well as the governor. It should conceive of its job as having these two distinct parts. As governor, the board should decide as a group upon the Ends that are desired and the means that are not. As workforce, individual members or work committees become board-assigned workers who clearly know the parameters of their particular jobs. Operating this way keeps the various parts (on-site work by committees or individuals) pulling toward the same aims (as decided by the board acting as a whole).

If your board has decided to use Policy Governance, and it does not have a CEO, it should:

- Notice that even though board members do much of the staff-like work, deciding what the organization is for and making it happen are two separate roles.
- Never allow the immediacy of *what* is to be done to distract them from their ongoing duty to decide *why* things should be done.
- Hold its members accountable for the jobs they were assigned.

Organizations with Small Staffs

When we work with the boards of small organizations, board members are often concerned that their staff is too small for the job. This is often an economic reality. Accordingly, they fear that being "a policy board" will result in the staff having inadequate human resources to do the job. We tell them that while staff likely do need help or advice, if staff are held accountable for achieving the Ends prescribed by the board within the latitude granted by the Executive Limitations policies, they will figure out for themselves what sort of help or advice they need. They can also decide where to get the help; in fact, because they may freely chose their help, they can still be held accountable for the decisions they make. Nothing in the Policy Governance model prevents a staff member from asking an individual board member to serve as a staff helper or adviser. The model does, however, prevent a board from foisting its help or advice on a largely defenseless staff. Board members who are asked by staff to provide a helpful or advisory service should remember that they are doing so not as board members but as individuals holding no power in the organization.

If your board has decided to use Policy Governance, it should:

- Make Ends ambitious, but be realistic about resources available to you.
- Understand that the board as a body exists not to help staff but to govern.

- Leave staff the prerogative of choosing to use board members as volunteer helpers, if board members wish to help.
- Remember that if the staff require help, they can ask for it.

Externally Required Approvals

State or provincial governments, funders, regulators, and accreditors often require that boards approve various pieces of staff work. This requirement regularly applies to budgets, program plans, and in the case of school boards, hirings. Of course, budgets, plans, and hirings are staff means issues. Such requirements stem from antiquated notions of proper board behavior that, unfortunately, are still the norm among funders, regulators, and accrediting bodies. It is altogether fitting, of course, for a funder, regulator, or accreditor to demand evidence that the board is actually in charge, that it is, in fact, governing. But as persons familiar with Policy Governance understand, traditional approvals signify just the opposite; they are a trivialized form of leadership without its substance, usually more akin to institutionalized tinkering than governing.

So what should the board do when an outside authority requires what is, in fact, poorer governance than the board would otherwise conduct? The answer is simple. Comply. Not to do so may endanger a grant or break the law. We are not advising, however, that the board revert to a process of painstakingly examining documents with no criteria to compare them to. The following sequence should occur: Ahead of time, the board will have required the CEO to inform it that an approval is required by an outside authority on a matter that is within the CEO's domain, that is, a decision not denied to the CEO by Executive Limitations policies. The CEO demonstrates to the board (in a monitoring report attached to the item to be approved) that the CEO's decision on the matter is in compliance with board policy. (See sample monitoring report in Resource C.) If the board is assured that the item does not violate its policy, it then approves the item as a consent agenda action. The only legitimate board discussion to take place at this point would be, if any is needed at all, (1) to question the monitoring assurance if applicable or (2) to call the applicable board policy into question. Individual members of the board are not allowed to pull the item off the consent agenda simply because they want to engage in helping make or change the decision.

If your board has decided to use Policy Governance, it should:

- Expect greater accountability of itself than is possible by ritual approvals.
- Be explicit about the values it would have used in deciding approval or disapproval.
- Refuse to allow outside authorities to deter it from responsible governance.
- Comply with outside authorities, but by using meaningful methods.

Board Meetings

Board meetings conducted by Policy Governance boards differ from the board meetings many of us are used to. Traditionally, board meetings have been used to hear staff reports, approve committee recommendations and staff documents, or discuss issues that one or more board members have found important or interesting. It is usually difficult to find examples of boards discussing and deciding issues of Ends, or to see clarification of the values that lead to approvals of anything.

Moreover, the agenda of a traditional board is usually put together largely by the CEO. That is, management is deciding the matters to be discussed by the board. Is it any wonder that the board discusses issues of management rather than governance? We are not blaming CEOs for this, since they are doing what the board expects. We would point out, however, that this may be the only example in enterprise wherein the job of the superior is defined and stage-managed by the subordinate.

Policy Governance boards understand that they have a job to do that is different from the CEO's job. Indeed, the board job *precedes* that of the CEO, since the board defines the CEO's accountabilities. (In the beginning, there was the board—*not* the CEO.) The job outputs of a governing board are (1) linkage with the owners, (2) written governing policies, and (3) assurance of CEO-organizational performance. These products form the basis of the board's ongoing agenda. This may seem unusual, for we are accustomed to seeing board agendas crowded with someone else's job. Policy Governance boards spend their meetings doing their own jobs, and use their job description as the basis for annually or biannually planning board meetings.

The Policy Governance board meeting is planned as a single but integrated part of an ongoing job. We advise boards to plan their jobs for the next one to two years by deciding what they want to have accomplished at the end of that period. If a board decides that it wishes to have made policy decisions about Ends at the end of the period, it may also decide that in order to do so, it must hold discussions about Ends with various pressure groups, community groups, governments, community boards, futurists, or demographers. Such consultations must be planned. The board must decide the items it most needs input about from these groups, and make sure that the groups know the questions they are being called upon to answer. A one- or two-year work plan emerges from such an approach, and while the chair will likely prepare the meeting-by-meeting agendas, they will be based on (any reasonable interpretation of) the work plan produced by the board.

Accordingly, a given board meeting may contain few or no decisions, with the preponderance of meeting time being spent on education and preparation for major Ends decision making at a future time. Board meetings have only minimal concern with immediate activities of the organization. These activities are monitored against policy criteria, but the monitoring data are usually only discussed in the meeting in the event that the data show policy nonachievement or violation.

The agenda of a typical board meeting in Policy Governance can vary quite as much as an agenda of any other board. The principles of governance are the same from one Policy Governance board to another, but the meeting content and format can vary widely. Let us offer a sample agenda (Exhibit 3.1) for illustration only; our comments are in brackets.

Board Members

It is very common for boards to recruit new members with the intent of duplicating skills needed at the staff level of organization. Hence boards become stocked with well-meaning people who

Exhibit 3.1. Sample Board Meeting Agenda.

Youth, Inc.

Board Meeting Agenda

Date

1. CALL TO ORDER

2. MINUTES: Approval of the minutes of previous meeting *[It is important for the board to declare its official record. The board secretary then signs the minutes form as having been so certified by board vote on this date.]*

3. MONITORING AFFIRMATION: Board members individually affirm that they have received and read all monitoring reports since last meeting *[Monitoring need not consume precious meeting time, but it is important that the board be sure its members are carrying out their out-of-meeting duty to read the periodic performance data.]*

4. ENDS: Meeting with Association of Concerned Parents to discuss the needs of parents of imprisoned youth *[The board would spend a lot of its time being educated about issues relevant to its ongoing cycle of reviewing and revising Ends policies.]*

5. GOVERNANCE PROCESS: Decision on the questions to be mailed to Probation and Parole Department in advance of January meeting. *[Asking for "input" in a general way can be useless. This board is honing just what it needs to learn from this source.]*

6. CONSENT AGENDA: Approval of application for state funds for next year's budget. Monitoring report attached. *[The board has put actual budget details into the CEO's hands so long as the budget is consistent with a reasonable interpretation of the board's policy on budgeting. There is no reason for the budget to be on the agenda except that the state requires board approval. The monitoring report attached gives the board the confidence it needs to go ahead with what amounts to a ritual approval.]*

7. NEXT MEETING *[Here the board reviews where it is in the annual cycle of board leadership, with special emphasis on what preparation is necessary for the next meeting.]*

8. SELF-EVALUATION: Board member Sam Jones will compare this meeting with Governance Process policy "Governance Style" *[This board rotates among its members the responsibility for formal assessment of each meeting, using a different board means policy each time.]*

9. ADJOURNMENT

believe, for good reason, that they are on the board in order to help with, assess, instruct about, or in some way be involved in staff work. New Policy Governance boards need to learn that their job breaks radically from this practice and that the skills they need to bring to the meeting may differ greatly from those they brought before. It is our experience that most board members can make this transition well, and in many cases they are relieved to be spending their time discussing and deciding issues that make a real difference.

Some board members, a minority, find the change entirely disagreeable. They enjoy being involved in the day-to-day workings of the organization and wish to continue to be so involved. Such board members would do well to vacate their board position and apply for volunteer work in the organization. Both service-level and governance-level volunteers are valuable to the organization. The difference is a matter of aptitude and interest, not one of moral superiority of one over the other.

It is also common to see boards appoint members based on their membership in designated groups. These are often called *constituency board members,* since there is an expectation that these persons represent the views of the particular group of which they are a member. Thus "student reps" on college boards, or "consumer reps" on social service or health boards are given the unenviable task of voicing the point of view of a community of people who do not have just one point of view.

Sometimes seats on boards have been created for persons who by tradition have been systematically excluded from governing positions, and we are sympathetic to the desire to put right this injustice. Our concern however is twofold. First, this method of appointing board members constituency-by-constituency will always exclude some group. Thus the desire to be inclusive results in exclusivity. Second, this method unfairly typecasts the board member. We would like all members of the board to see themselves as standing in for all of the owners. Recognizing that there will rarely be enough diversity on the board to represent the diversity in the ownership, the board as a whole should reach out to include input from those who are not on the board.

An additional word about consumer reps may be useful. The most time-consuming and difficult job of the board is the determining of organizational Ends. Ends include the designation of the consumers of the benefits to be produced by the organization. Today's consumers may be able to help greatly in such a designation, but it is important to remember that the most responsible decision may be that today's consumers are not those who should be tomorrow's consumers. This makes the job of board member particularly difficult for consumer reps.

Boards are organs of ownership, *not* organs of customership or of any of the several other stakeholder groups. It is not that the board doesn't care about, say, consumers or staff, but that consumers and staff, insofar as those roles are concerned, are not owners. We urge consumer reps or staff reps on boards (put there by law or other requirement) to refuse to accept the tokenism this practice implies and to take upon themselves the same wide-ranging portfolio of other board members, that is, to represent the entire ownership. Moreover, we warn boards that their obligation to reach out in some systematic way to the entire ownership is not lessened because they have "representatives" of certain constituencies on the board.

Officially designated as a constituency member or not, every board member is from somewhere. Governance would work better if designated constituency members were considered to be *from* a constituency rather than to *represent* it. Hence, a woman on a board doesn't represent all women, nor does a person of color represent all persons of color. To so construe the role is disrespectful to the wide heterogeneity within these descriptions. Having a person from a certain neighborhood on the board does not excuse the board from designing strategies of reaching out to that neighborhood just as energetically as if no one from the neighborhood were on the board. Sometimes the tokenism effect of having constituency board members actually thwarts the result that was intended.

Policy Governance requires board members who are interested in and capable of discussing the values underlying the actions taken every day in the organization and governing through the broader formulations of these values. Hence board members should enjoy conceptual argument, differing points of view, and values clarification. They should understand that they stand in for an ownership of diverse people who have many legitimate points of view, and they should actively seek to access and understand that diversity. They should welcome dissent but be able to honor group decisions once they are made.

If your board has decided to use Policy Governance, it should:

- Remember that its job is not to help the staff.
- Protect its staff from board members who wish to manage the organization without having gone through the formality of being hired.
- Recruit people who are interested in the difficult task of Ends determination.
- Encourage the expression of dissent in board discussion.
- Deliberate with many voices but govern with one in instructing the CEO.
- Remember that the diversity of the organization's ownership is larger than can be represented directly by any board.
- Seek to link with the ownership in as inclusive a way as possible, regardless of whether there are constituency members on the board.

Board Discipline

Even highly disciplined individuals have trouble acting as part of a disciplined group. Yet a disciplined group is exactly what a board of directors must be. Boards must decide on a method to use in governing, and use it. They must decide what the group expectations are about such matters as attendance, individual use of authority, preparation for meetings, and conflict of interest, and then enforce them. We have often seen boards make statements about their intentions in governance but fail to police themselves when they don't meet those expectations. It is as if the statement of intention suffices to fulfill the discipline. That doesn't work for dieting or mowing the lawn—and it won't work for governance.

The board chair has a special responsibility for board discipline but is not the only enforcer. Group discipline simply works better if all the board members agree to help each other maintain the standards the board has set. Governance Process policies spell out board expectations in this regard and should be used as the criteria against which board performance is regularly assessed by the board.

The board as a body has an additional responsibility to protect its staff from the board as individuals. This is done by instituting a policy stating that the CEO, while accountable to the board for complying with policies produced by the board, is not accountable for pleasing board members as individuals.

If your board has decided to use Policy Governance, it should:

- Formally commit to observing the policies it has set for itself.
- Enforce the agreed-upon rules when they are violated by board members.
- Understand that being part of a disciplined board makes an individual's attempted exercise of governing powers illegitimate.
- Support the chair when this officer undertakes to ensure group discipline.

Board Orientation

Too often, board orientation, if it happens at all, is an exercise in teaching board members about everybody's job but their own. Organizations ordinarily orient new members far more about what staff members are doing than about what the board's specific job is and how it does it. The Policy Governance model needs to be known and understood in order to be used. New board members, and even experienced ones, need to be continually refreshed in their knowledge of the model. Using experienced members to instruct new members will keep both better educated. Governance discussions and reading relevant materials are two more ways of ensuring that the topic of governance remains on the board's agenda.

If your board has decided to use Policy Governance, it should:

- Ensure that new board members know the method of governance used by the board before they join the board if possible, but in any event, as soon as they join.
- Use the principles of the model so that it is obvious that problem solving within the model enables and forces clarity.
- Ensure that the policies are up-to-date, frequently reviewed, and immediately updated after any change.

Board Officers and Committees

If your board is to govern as a group and speak with one voice, it must avoid some time-honored practices with regard to officers and committees.

Officers are traditionally given responsibilities that duplicate those given to the CEO. We have previously discussed the common practice of delegating portions of CEO responsibility to the treasurer, the chair, and to a variety of committees. While this practice is contrary to Policy Governance principles, we do not mean to imply that there can be no valid role for officers or committees. Nor do we mean that board members with special expertise cannot be valuable in assisting other board members' understanding. A financial expert, for example, can be useful in assisting the board to craft its policies related to finances (though there is no reason that person needs to hold an office). The chair plays an essential and authoritative role in Policy Governance but should not have authority in the CEO's domain.

Traditionally, we have learned to speak of boards and committees much as we speak of peaches and cream or horses and carriages; they go together. People have a hard time conceiving of a board without committees. This is regrettable. Some boards never need a committee and, in any event, there is *no* committee that is generically necessary to governance. Moreover, people often have a clearer, albeit misinformed, notion of what certain familiar committees should do than they have of what the board should do. Yet, since a committee is a subpart of the board, the role or even the need for any committee cannot possibly be determined until the role of the board as a whole has been decided.

We warn you about a particularly harmful committee—the executive committee—for it uniquely undermines both board and CEO authority. Since an executive committee is usually granted the authority to make board decisions when the board is not in session, its authority may in practice be more far-reaching than that of the board itself. Moreover, it inserts itself between the board and the CEO, making it difficult to tell exactly for whom the CEO works. Board members not on the executive committee often feel excluded from the real decision making and unable to control the committee's activities, even though board committees are ostensibly subservient to the board. Indeed, we have almost never seen standards of performance or clear descriptions of the responsibility of executive committees, even though we have seen them make the majority of decisions. On the other hand, a board feels relieved of much of its burden when it defaults to a committee in this way. A Policy Governance board must forego the illusion of efficiency provided by a traditional executive committee.

If your board has decided to use Policy Governance, it should:

- Create no office or committee position for the purpose of helping, advising, instructing, or exercising responsibility for or authority over any aspect of organization that has been delegated to the CEO.
- Use committees, if it wishes, to help the board with parts of its job.
- Allow no committee to be a board-within-the-board.
- Create committees that last as long as the job the committee has to do, but no longer.
- Be clear about the product the board is requiring from the committee (for example, advice to the board or a set of options for board action).
- Be clear about the resources the committee is authorized to use (for example, money or staff time).
- Use the expertise of board members to inform but not substitute for board wisdom.

We can assume, then, that your board has learned the theory, is committed to continually getting more clear about it, and has considered and accepted the implications of governing through the Policy Governance model. As you get started, it will be instructive to remember that implementing the model is a capital investment in your capability to govern, not just a board training exercise. It calls for a little extra work but saves unnecessary work in the long run. It calls for attention to what might look like housekeeping but grants you freedom from much of the housekeeping afterward. Most of all, you will be laying the framework in which your leadership can be expressed.

Next Chapter

At this point, we have completed your preparation. Be prepared to come back to Part One or to the other Policy Governance publications to clear up any remaining issues about theory whenever you need to do so. You will find, in fact, that occasional discussions of the theory alone will help keep your implementation focused.

In Chapter Four, we help you to examine the creation of Executive Limitations policies, those board policies that put off-limits certain organizational practices, decisions, activities, methods, and situations. These policies in effect put a fence around the CEO and his or her subordinates within which they may make whatever decisions they deem fitting. Now, let's get into the work of Policy Governance.

Crafting Policies

Part Two consists of four chapters in modified workbook form. We guide you through the establishment of board policies in the four Policy Governance categories. Because the Policy Governance model relies so much on explicit statements of board values and on carefully following the new policy-making principles, creating those policies is a fundamental part of implementation. In fact, a board cannot be said to have implemented the model if the policies are not in place; intent and even a change of mentality are not enough.

Chapter Four

Executive Limitations Policies

Restricting the CEO's Choices

In this chapter, we guide you through the formulation of Executive Limitations policies—those policies enabling the board to withdraw safely from most details of operation. On the circle diagram introduced in Chapter Two, these policies are located and will control everything in the lower right-hand quadrant (see Figure 4.1). Policy Governance cannot be implemented unless these policies are in place. They are the board's way of telling the CEO the limits of acceptability regarding staff means (methods, situations, circumstances, and practices). Thus these policies are boundary setters. It is not necessary that you call them Executive Limitations, of course, but it is important that your title for this category of board policy indicate the limiting, constraining, or restrictive nature of these documents. Examples would be Operational Parameters, CEO Authority Limits, Administrative Boundaries, or even Unacceptable Operational Situations and Actions.

Executive Limitations policies, just as Ends policies, are addressed to the CEO, not to the entire staff. While Ends policies tell the CEO what the board intends for the organization to achieve, the Executive Limitations policies tell the CEO what the board will not put up with. The CEO will be held personally accountable that all staff means fall within the boundaries established by the Executive Limitations policies. The idea of boundary setting is important for establishing optimal delegation. For the board to get the most out of its staff, it is necessary to give the staff a great deal of

Figure 4.1. The Staff Means Quadrant.

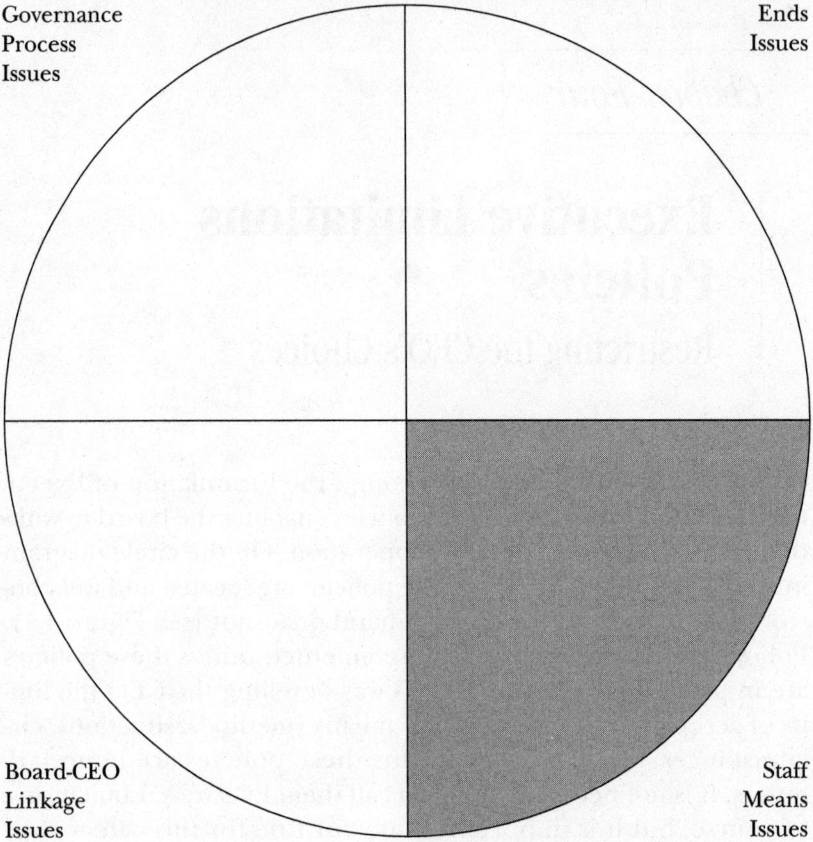

Governance
Process
Issues

Ends
Issues

Board-CEO
Linkage
Issues

Staff
Means
Issues

Note: On the circle diagram introduced in Chapter Two, the issues dealt with in this chapter are in the lower right-hand quadrant.

room to make decisions. This is best done by giving total authority in a blanket kind of way but pulling some of it back in selected ways. This is accomplished by the negatively worded policies, for it is the Executive Limitations policies that do this pulling back and thereby establish the latitude of your CEO's authority.

It may be useful to think of Executive Limitations policies as establishing the conditions for *pre-approval* of any staff decisions or activities that do not violate the policies. Thus if budgets, compensation plans, or other operational decisions are not in violation of Executive Limitation policies, they are automatically board-authorized. It is as if the board says to the CEO, "Any action you take or situation you get into can be considered board-approved if it does not violate our policies." These policies allow boards to take care of their worries about staff activities by defining those worries and explicitly proscribing them. Like all policy making in the Policy Governance model, the creation of Executive Limitations policies starts at the most general, most inclusive level (the outside edge of the quadrant), and then policies are further defined until that point at which any remaining reasonable interpretation by the CEO would be acceptable to the board. At this point, delegation occurs. The board holds the CEO accountable for ensuring that all further decisions and actions *do* constitute reasonable interpretations.

As you create Executive Limitations policies, at each stage you will be asking yourself whether you can accept any reasonable interpretation of your words by the CEO. We urge you to decide this question *based not on your guess about your incumbent CEO's likely interpretation* but based upon your comfort with the entire range of interpretation allowed by your words. In other words, you will be making policies with *your own values* in mind, not your predictions about your current CEO. This will give your policies a durability that will outlive any given CEO. It will also avoid the disillusionment that leads to a board's subsequent lament to the effect that the CEO "didn't do what we assumed she would, given our previous knowledge of her."

Before we begin, let us clear up an impediment that causes many boards to hang up in this process. Do not confuse the task of policy making with the task of monitoring policy performance. The best policy—contrary to what is often said—will be created by completely ignoring how it will be evaluated. It is important that the board be true to itself and its values by clearly enunciating, in the case of Executive Limitations, the boundaries of prudence and ethics to which it commits the organization. If you combine that task with contriving measurement methods, you will warp the clarification of your values in the service of easier measurement. Therefore, as you enter upon the work of this chapter, simply take for granted that monitoring will be done acceptably. That is, *assume* that if you say the CEO shall not wear brown shoes, a way will be devised to determine whether brown shoes are worn. Now, let's get on with Executive Limitations policies!

Let's Take It from the Top: Level One

So, in answer to the question what should we tell the CEO not to do or allow, we should be drafting the most general, most inclusive, largest-mixing-bowl policy that the board can start with. In our experience assisting many boards with this process, we have found that a statement similar to the following is a good place to start. Because it is the first and broadest level of Executive Limitations, for reference in our step-by-step approach we refer to this statement of policy as EL #1.

Policy EL #1: Global Executive Limitations Policy

The CEO shall not cause or allow any practice, activity, decision, or organizational circumstance that is either unlawful, imprudent, or in violation of commonly accepted business and professional ethics.

Some boards find that their special circumstances require them to make this policy more inclusive. For example, a Catholic hospital board may add "violation of canonical law," or a national Red Cross board may add "violation of the principles of the international Red Cross and Red Crescent movement." Many nonprofit boards dependent on grant funds add "violation of regulations of funding agencies or regulatory bodies." Remember that the board's task at this stage (EL #1) is to find policy wording that is of sufficient breadth to include *all* possible actions that it would find unacceptable. Breadth is the point here, not depth. Depth will be considered later as we expand upon this statement, but we must first have a statement of sufficient integrity and inclusiveness to support the expansions.

Some board members will see no value in stating such a broad proscription, feeling that if a board has to tell its CEO not to break the law, it has the wrong CEO. They are right of course, as far as that goes. But the point of Executive Limitations policy making is to leave no holes in the understanding a board has with its CEO. Having a broad statement as the foundation for further detailed statements means that if the board overlooks a subsequent, more detailed prohibition, there is always the broader one to fall back upon. Therefore, expect some board members to complain that this broadest Executive Limitations statement is very broad and nonspecific, leaving a great deal open to interpretation. *This is exactly the point.*

ASSIGNMENT: Discuss the broad Executive Limitations policy (EL #1) and decide what language would serve best for your board. Be careful not to prescribe means, and be careful not to go into more detail.

You have now created the outermost policy within the Executive Limitations category of board policies, as shown in Figure 4.2. Although you will likely go into more detail, you have covered most of your worries with this simple policy standing alone. Most of the trouble that nonprofit and governmental organizations get themselves into results from violations of this one-sentence policy.

Although we have never encountered the situation, a board could stop at this EL #1 level of policy making, thereby delegating to its CEO the broad latitude that stopping at this point would leave. In any event, either to continue or to conclude the process of Executive Limitations policy making, your board must ask itself

Figure 4.2. Executive Limitations, Level One.

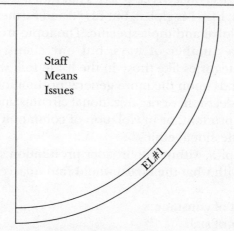

Note: At this point in our exercise, the outer level of the policy circle has been completed in the Executive Limitations portion. Executive means have now been contained, even if at a broad level.

the question, Can we accept *any reasonable interpretation* of these words from our CEO? A board agreeing to accept the CEO's interpretation at this stage has nothing further to say about the means of staff. Its Executive Limitations policy making is over. (It will, however, have to monitor whether staff means do indeed respect the boundaries placed on them by this policy.)

If, as we suspect, your board is not willing to entrust your CEO with the interpretation (no matter how reasonable his or her interpretations might be) of so broad a statement, then there is more Executive Limitations work to be done. The reason, of course, is that if your board is not comfortable leaving Executive Limitations at the broadest level, it means that the board has worries *within* even reasonable interpretations of that broadest level. The next task for your board, then, will be to go into more detail about prohibitions than you have already stated in broad terms in EL #1. We'll call this next level of detail EL #2.

Here's a Little More Detail: Going to Level Two

There was only one statement to be made at the EL #1 level, for by its nature EL #1 addresses the entire spectrum of all possible staff actions and situations. When a board chooses to go into more detail, however, its concerns or worries fall into a number of subject areas. That is, EL #1 is global, but EL #2 and further levels are necessarily subglobal and topic-specific. The topic areas could be organized in a number of ways, but our clients have typically employed categories like those in the list to follow. Each, you will notice, expands upon the more general prohibition against "practice, activity, decision, or organizational circumstance that is either unlawful, imprudent, or in violation of commonly accepted business and professional ethics."

These topics, within the broader prohibition stated by EL #1, might deal with what the board would find unacceptable about:

- Treatment of consumers
- Treatment of staff
- Financial planning and budgeting
- Financial condition and activities
- Emergency CEO succession

- Asset protection
- Compensation and benefits
- Communication and support to the board

At this stage, it may be helpful to pause and consider what re-actions you have to the list of unacceptables. We sympathize with the intuitive reaction that such a starkly negative list is off-putting. But we encourage you to reflect on what this establishes in your delegation of operational means to your CEO: if the board hasn't said the CEO can't, the CEO can. Anything the CEO decides to do, except those things prohibited, is acceptable. This delegation ap-proach is extremely empowering but cannot work without a stark delineation of what is out of bounds. If we soften the language of what is unacceptable, we risk throwing the massive empowerment into question.

As we take your board through a consideration of Executive Limitations policies of greater depth than EL #1, we will use the foregoing topics simply because we have found them most useful for most organizations. There is no reason that your board could not create policies organized into different groupings than these. For example, a school board the senior author worked with some years ago saw fit to include at least two aspects of the list shown under a single "unacceptable treatment of people" policy. Further, some boards, due to the unique nature of their organization or en-vironment, will develop policies with content unlike any of these (though the format and principles will be identical). To illustrate, as we get into the EL #2 level, we will include a policy that would be specific to grant-making organizations (such as foundations) or ones that contract out services to other organizations. Such a pol-icy may be necessary to ensure that an ends focus is maintained even when outside vendors are utilized.

So at this next level (EL #2), the board articulates further pol-icy language regarding any area of concern for which it feels a need to narrow the broader language of EL #1. Although policies at this next level are more detailed than at the EL #1 level, they will be the most general policies within the chosen categories, that is, the broadest proscription about financial management that is more detailed than what appears already in EL #1. (Note that fi-nancial management is covered by EL #1 already, even though it

isn't even mentioned there by name.) It is important to keep the
EL #2 proscriptions at the EL #2 level, for tempted though it may
be, the board should not prematurely plunge into detail in any
area. Rather it should proceed level by level.

Proceeding through the list just shown, we will guide you
through examples of policies developed by our clients. Each area
addressed is assigned a letter suffix. Accordingly, the policy about
the treatment of consumers is referred to as EL #2a and the policy
about treatment of staff as EL #2b. Remember that these policies
are not being offered as best for any particular organization but
simply as examples of policies that are consistent with Policy Governance principles. A particular board may use some or all of the
policy subject areas and may change many or few of the words.

Let us say a word about our organization of this material. We
are taking you through a level-by-level examination of your values,
as they relate to the boundaries of acceptable staff situations and
actions. In subsequent chapters, we take the same cascading-level
approach in the other policy categories. We are about to begin
dealing with various topics at Level Two within Executive Limitations. We are, therefore, addressing *policies by topics within each level.*

However, when the policies are complete, using them efficiently calls for putting all the levels about one topic together so
they can be followed easily. In this way board criteria about the
same topic are not scattered. In Part Three when we deal with
maintaining Policy Governance, we revisit this issue and demonstrate what the completed actual policies look like. In Resource A,
we assemble the various levels of policies on their various topics
into the format used in a completed policy manual. For now, however, we enter our level-by-level treatment, one topic at a time.

ASSIGNMENT: Go through each of the following EL #2 statements
in turn, taking your time to discuss whether some or all of each
make sense to your board. Resist going into more detail than this
now. Also, resist the temptation to word-craft commas and semicolons and grammar. Instead, examine your differences of opinion
about the values expressed. Don't forget that each consideration
that follows will have been preceded by the more general prohibition of the EL #1 statement. Hence, it would be unnecessary to
state not to break the law with respect to, say, treatment of consumers. Further, as we remind you as we go along, failing to cover

a topic at the EL #2 level does not mean the board will have no control over that topic. It simply means that the control will be the broader (one might say, looser) control about that topic imposed by the proscriptive language in your global, EL #1 policy.

Policy EL #2a: Treatment of Consumers

With respect to interactions with consumers or those applying to be consumers, the CEO shall not cause or allow conditions, procedures, or decisions that are unsafe, undignified, unnecessarily intrusive, or that fail to provide appropriate confidentiality or privacy.

Remember that the *benefits* to be produced for consumers, as well as the identification of the consumers, are ends matters and are not at issue here. This policy merely establishes that the organization's interaction with consumers may not violate the principles stated. Does this policy state your board's values with respect to treatment of consumers? If you are a hospital board or city council, would "*unduly* undignified" be better than simply "undignified" because of the nature of your organization's work? The best medical and police activity, for example, can incur some unavoidably undignified situations.

If a board were to use wording such as that shown in this policy, it would again raise the question as to whether it can accept any reasonable interpretation of these words by the CEO. For example, a range of interpretations could reasonably be given to the words *undignified, intrusive, appropriate,* and even *privacy* and *consumers.* If only a part of that range is acceptable, then these words are insufficient to describe what the board intends.

ASSIGNMENT: Discuss this policy and decide whether it is needed at all, establishes sufficient control, or needs further definition. Deciding that it is not needed means the board is satisfied for the CEO to be limited only by the broader language of EL #1 with respect to this topic. If this EL #2 policy provides necessary and sufficient control, the CEO will have the right to use any reasonable interpretation of its narrower language. If still greater control of CEO options is needed, further definition of this EL #2 policy is required. Consider the examples of EL #3 policies shown later in this chapter.

Policy EL #2b: Treatment of Staff

With respect to the treatment of paid and volunteer staff, the CEO may not cause or allow conditions that are unfair or undignified.

Let us remind you again that all policies at EL #2 (and further) are contained within the general proscription of EL #1. Hence, boards that are concerned about the laws relating to staff treatment, as well as about collective agreements, should recall that the CEO has already been placed under a general instruction that the violation of *any law* or any legally binding agreement (general prudence and ethics) will not be permitted. In fact, unless the board's proscriptions about treatment of staff go further than law and business ethics, there is no need for this policy at all, even at the EL #2 level.

It is important to note that however detailed the board may get in its policy making, when it does delegate, it delegates to the CEO. Hence, in the case of this policy, definition of the words *unfair* and *undignified* is the prerogative of the CEO, not of staff members.

ASSIGNMENT: Discuss and decide whether this policy is needed at all, establishes sufficient control, or needs further definition. Deciding that it is not needed means the board is satisfied for the CEO to be limited only by the broader language of EL #1 with respect to this topic. If this EL #2 policy provides necessary and sufficient control, the CEO will have the right to use any reasonable interpretation of its narrower language. If still greater control of CEO options is needed, further definition of this EL #2 policy is required. Consider the examples of EL #3 policies shown later in this chapter.

Policy EL #2c: Financial Planning and Budgeting

Financial planning for any fiscal year or the remaining part of any fiscal year shall not deviate materially from the board's Ends priorities, risk fiscal jeopardy, or fail to be derived from a multiyear plan.

This policy acknowledges that the most important aspect of a budget is that it enables the accomplishment of ends in proper proportionality. (Conventional line-item budgets do not demonstrate the link between Ends priorities and financial allocations.)

The policy also acknowledges that the CEO will be engaged in financial planning on a virtually continual basis. Hence its proscription applies on a year-round basis. Contrast this with the fiction maintained by many boards that financial planning occurs only once per year and results in one budget that the board must approve (against unstated criteria). Here, the board states a proscription that requires the CEO to maintain integrity in fiscal planning *however often budgets are updated.*

Note that the wording indicates only three interests the board has in budgeting (beyond the global interest imbedded in the EL #1 policy). Is this true for your board? What other interests are there beyond mere, but understandable, curiosity? This is not the time to concern yourself with those aspects of budget that the board merely wants to know about (rather than to control). At this point the board is setting criteria for performance, which is a very different undertaking than listing what it would like to know about. So be careful not to confuse curiosity with giving direction. Since these are the only criteria (perhaps to be augmented later by Level Three or beyond), any budgeting your CEO does that is consistent with the policy that emerges here is automatically approvable.

ASSIGNMENT: Discuss this policy and decide whether it is needed at all, establishes sufficient control, or needs further definition. Deciding that it is not needed means the board is satisfied for the CEO to be limited only by the broader language of EL #1 with respect to this topic. If this EL #2 policy provides necessary and sufficient control, the CEO will have the right to use any reasonable interpretation of its narrower language. If still greater control of CEO options is needed, further definition of this EL #2 policy is required. Consider the examples of EL #3 policies shown later in this chapter.

Policy EL #2d: Financial Condition and Activities

With respect to the actual, ongoing financial conditions and activities, the CEO shall not cause or allow the development of fiscal jeopardy or a material deviation of actual expenditures from board priorities established in Ends policies.

Policy Governance boards commonly enact an Executive Limitations policy about *actual* financial situations, in addition to *intentions* about financial situations (budget). They acknowledge that despite the most skilled planning, the organization can still wander into an unacceptable position. Accordingly, the board here defines those fiscal conditions and activities that it would deem unacceptable. Indeed, actual financial condition and activities are far more important than budget, even though traditional boards place most of their financial emphasis on budgets. In fact, no organization ever went broke because of its budget; plenty have gone broke because of their actual financial condition! Thus the board has reason to worry far more about actual than about budget.

This policy should provoke a discussion by your board of the traditional practice of actual-to-budget comparisons as a way of reporting fiscal condition. While we are not dealing with the monitoring of these policies in this chapter, a digression on this matter is in order. One might ask, If the organization has a budget, why have a separate financial condition policy? Why not simply compare how the organization is doing to the budget? The reasons are twofold. First, if the board's expectation is that there be no deviation from budget at all, then every financial report will be out of compliance. If it is not to deviate from budget more than some percentage, why should the board assume that deviation in any amount is bad? Or is the organization not to deviate about certain aspects of budget, but others don't matter? Experienced, traditional boards know that separate judgments have to be made about deviations of different sorts. If separate judgments are made, upon what criteria are they made? We are back into making evaluative determinations against unstated criteria. In other words, that there is deviation is not very important. The question is still, What kinds of actual fiscal conditions or actions are unacceptable? These can be directly codified and placed in the Financial Condition and Activities policy.

Second, budget detail has been turned over to the CEO anyway. So the board has not decreed a set of specific numbers that the CEO must follow. The board has said that any budget the CEO wants to have is acceptable, as long as the provisions of the budget policy (shown earlier as EL #2c) are not breached. So comparing actual-to-budget merely tells the board how well the CEO is tracking with his or her own choice of budget numbers. This information is not a critical matter at the governance level. Besides, if the board's interest in financial planning has to do with its concern about integrity in planning the future, the only budget that addresses this concern is budgeting from the present, actual situation into the future—something the actual-to-budget comparison misses entirely!

Policy Governance calls upon your board to define (1) what it would not want to happen in budgeting (dealt with in EL #2c) and (2) what it would not want to occur in the organization's actual fiscal condition. This policy (EL #2d) provides your opportunity to settle the second question.

ASSIGNMENT: Discuss this policy and decide whether it is needed at all, establishes sufficient control, or needs further definition. Deciding that it is not needed means the board is satisfied for the CEO to be limited only by the broader language of EL #1 with respect to this topic. If this EL #2 policy provides necessary and sufficient control, the CEO will have the right to use any reasonable interpretation of its narrower language. If still greater control of CEO options is needed, further definition of this EL #2 policy is required. Consider the examples of EL #3 policies shown later in this chapter.

Policy EL #2e: Emergency CEO Succession

In order to protect the board from sudden loss of CEO services, the CEO may have no fewer than two other executives familiar with board and CEO issues and processes.

The board here is not requiring the CEO to name his or her successor. It is, however, requiring that in the event of a sudden loss of the existing CEO, there will be other staff members whom the board can ask to take over the helm while the board organizes its search for a replacement CEO. This policy does not deal with temporary absences, such as when the CEO is on vacation; the CEO is still CEO despite his or her absence. The CEO is accountable for the actions of those he or she has left in charge; the board needs no policy to deal with that continuing accountability.

Far more frequently than with the other EL #2-level policies in this discussion, our clients have regularly chosen not to go into further detail. If they did, they would be defining, for example, degrees of familiarity, which issues and processes are meant, and so forth. You, of course, may decide to do just that. On the other hand, what our clients ordinarily do is adjust the number of familiarized executives to be appropriate for the size of their organization.

ASSIGNMENT: Discuss this policy and decide whether it is needed at all, establishes sufficient control, or needs further definition. Deciding that it is not needed means the board is satisfied for the CEO to be limited only by the broader language of EL #1 with respect to this topic. If this EL #2 policy provides necessary and sufficient control, the CEO will have the right to use any reasonable interpretation of its narrower language. If still greater control of CEO options is needed, further definition of this EL #2 policy is required. We have not included an EL #3 policy on this topic, although you may choose one for your board.

Policy EL #2f: Asset Protection

The CEO shall not allow the assets to be unprotected, inadequately maintained, or unnecessarily risked.

The board legally possesses assets of different types. The board itself exercises little direct control over those assets, having by necessity put them under the care of the CEO. While the global Executive Limitations policy EL #1 requires general prudence about everything, this policy more specifically targets the stewardship of assets.

Notice that there are in this policy, as in all policies, many words that are open to interpretation. What is the definition of *asset?* Does it include nonmonetary goods, such as public image? What does *inadequately* mean? What is *unnecessary risk?*

ASSIGNMENT: Discuss this policy and decide whether it is needed at all, establishes sufficient control, or needs further definition. Deciding that it is not needed means the board is satisfied for the CEO to be limited only by the broader language of EL #1 with respect to this topic. If this EL #2 policy provides necessary and sufficient control, the CEO will have the right to use any reasonable interpretation of its narrower language. If still greater control of CEO options is needed, further definition of this EL #2 policy is required. Consider the examples of EL #3 policies shown later in this chapter.

Policy EL #2g: Compensation and Benefits

With respect to employment, compensation, and benefits to employees, consultants, contract workers, and volunteers, the CEO shall not cause or allow jeopardy to fiscal integrity or public image.

As written, this policy concentrates on two aspects of compensation and benefits: fiscal jeopardy and public image. Its message, which may or may not be the appropriate one for your board, is that beyond the basic proscription of EL #1, the board's only concern about compensation and benefits is that they not endanger the organization's fiscal health or cause a problem in the public's perception of the organization. As always, the board defines what would not be acceptable and allows the CEO to interpret its words.

ASSIGNMENT: Discuss this policy and decide whether it is needed at all, establishes sufficient control, or needs further definition. Deciding that it is not needed means the board is satisfied for the CEO to be limited only by the broader language of EL #1 with respect to this topic. If this EL #2 policy provides necessary and sufficient control, the CEO will have the right to use any reasonable interpretation of its narrower language. If still greater control of CEO options is needed, further definition of this EL #2 policy is required. Consider the examples of EL #3 policies shown later in this chapter.

Policy EL #2h: Communication and Support to the Board

The CEO shall not permit the board to be uninformed or unsupported in its work.

For a board to fulfill its role, it must have information that is likely to be in the hands of the staff, and it may need administrative support that the staff is best suited to provide. For example, a board may need legislative information or demographic data to which the staff has access. Or a board may need notices mailed, minutes prepared, and meeting rooms acquired. Certainly, a board needs information about performance from the staff when it has determined that staff is the preferred source of such information. Further, a board may simply want to know organizational information for personal or political reasons.

This policy says that board ignorance is one of the several unacceptable situations that the CEO is to avoid. As written at this EL #2 level, of course, the board isn't specific about all the kinds of information and support it wants. At this level, interpreting those things is left up to the CEO.

ASSIGNMENT: Discuss this policy and decide whether it is needed at all, establishes sufficient control, or needs further definition. Deciding that it is not needed means the board is satisfied for the CEO to be limited only by the broader language of EL #1 with respect to this topic. If this EL #2 policy provides necessary and sufficient control, the CEO will have the right to use any reasonable interpretation of its narrower language. If still greater control of CEO options is needed, further definition of this EL #2 policy is required. Consider the examples of EL #3 policies shown later in this chapter.

Policy EL #2i: Ends Focus of Grants or Contracts

The CEO may not enter into any grant or contract arrangements that fail to emphasize primarily the production of Ends and, secondarily, the avoidance of unacceptable means.

This policy would be considered by the board of an organization that funds other organizations, such as a foundation or governmental funding agency. It would also be considered by the board of an organization that contracts with other organizations for some portion of its Ends. It is included here to illustrate a policy that is not typical.

Policy Governance boards spend most of their time focusing on the Ends to be achieved by their organizations. It would seem incongruous to permit their organizations to fund other organizations in a way that forces a focus on means. The policy shown above requires a relationship between the funding organization and the contractor or vendor organization that is very different from that commonly seen in nonprofit and public arenas.

The policy forces the CEO's grant making to emphasize the performance of a grantee along lines of proper results for the intended recipients at the appropriate cost, rather than to intrude into the grantee's methods. Although requiring the "primary determinant" to be these Ends factors, the policy leaves the CEO room for a secondary focus on unacceptable means (such as discrimination, unsafe conditions, and so forth).

ASSIGNMENT: Discuss this policy and decide whether it is needed at all, establishes sufficient control, or needs further definition. Deciding that it is not needed means the board is satisfied for the CEO to be limited only by the broader language of EL #1 with respect to this topic. If this EL #2 policy provides necessary and sufficient control, the CEO will have the right to use any reasonable interpretation of its narrower language. If still greater control of CEO options is needed, further definition of this EL #2 policy is required. Consider the examples of EL #3 policies shown later in this chapter.

Let's Check the Map to See Where We Are

Now let's see where all this Level Two work has gotten you. Figure 4.3 indicates the "thicker" sealing of the boundary of acceptability formed by these more detailed policies. The effect is to restrict the CEO's potential choices in operating the organization to a greater degree than was possible at Level One. The Level Two controls, of course, may or may not be sufficient. For those areas in which they are insufficient, we next demonstrate going to the next level of detail (EL #3).

The institution of EL #2 policies narrows the latitude left to the CEO by the board in EL #1. Further definition by the board of its EL #2 words, if it chooses to do it, will again narrow this latitude. We are not encouraging either going into more detail or staying out of it. We are, however, urging your board to be honest about the matter. If the board is truthfully not going to allow the CEO the entire range of reasonable interpretation of the EL #2 policies, it is duty bound to provide further definition. The board that eschews greater detail, yet is perfectly willing to make judgments

Figure 4.3. Executive Limitations, Levels One and Two.

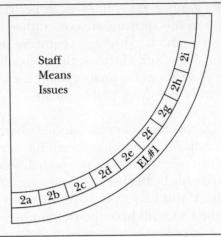

Staff
Means
Issues

2a 2b 2c 2d 2e 2f 2g 2h 2i EL#1

Note: With policy language at the EL #2 level, the initial, global proscription of staff means has been extended into topic-specific areas.

about those unstated details, will damage its CEO's trust and its own integrity.

ASSIGNMENT: Look over your work so far. You have now created one EL #1 global policy and several further defined constraints on the CEO at the EL #2 level. The CEO is bound by all these taken together. Does your board have any worries about staff methods, practices, and situations that are not covered by these statements? Remember that you will have further opportunity to make the policies more specific, but these should provide the foundation upon which any further specifics are based.

You will notice in our diagram (Figure 4.3) that the EL #2 policies do not completely cover the arc. We have left that gap to symbolize some further defining at Level Two that the board has either accidentally or intentionally omitted. Such omission is possible because no board can think of everything right at the beginning of its Policy Governance implementation. But the principle of logical containment, illustrated by the "coming in on the circle" scheme of policies, ensures that at whatever level the board's omission occurs, the safety net about staff means merely drops back to the next larger level. It never falls all the way through as if there were no policy protection at all.

Going into Even More Detail: Level Three

The previous policy language gives the CEO a comfortable latitude for decision making, perhaps more latitude in some areas than your board wishes. Assume for a moment that your CEO consistently uses a reasonable interpretation of these policies and can demonstrate to the board that he or she has done so. Would it then be possible for the CEO still to do or allow things that, while consistent with your policies, are still not acceptable to the board? If not, your Executive Limitations policy making is complete. You can stop. If so, there is still more policy crafting to do. A third level of detail will be necessary for one or more of the topics already covered.

In the following pages of this chapter, we demonstrate some Level Three policies (EL #3). These take the words of the Level Two policies and further define them. Remember that Level Two policies are themselves built upon the Level One policy that started this sequence. For example, your board does not need to repeat the proscription about breaking the law, since this was included at Level One. Also remember—we are not recommending that any board go into the level of detail shown or that boards should exceed it. That is the board's decision. Policy Governance provides a framework for effectively codifying your board's values; it does not dictate what the content or breadth of those values will be.

So let's return to the same policies you have just completed and consider taking their proscriptions into the next level of detail. At this point you may have changed the language of these EL #2 policies to fit your own values. Since we can't know what changes you made, we proceed using the samples with which we began.

Earlier we pointed out that EL #1 is global and is, therefore, a single statement standing alone. When you drop below the global level, that is, when you go into more detail with EL #2, there are a number of parallel topics. We illustrated several as EL #2a, EL #2b, and so forth. Similarly, you could see each of the EL #2 policies as global within its topic area, so that going into the level of EL #3 will produce a number of parallel items within each of the EL #2 topics. That is what you will see as we take the next step.

ASSIGNMENT: For each of the EL #2 policies that in the previous exercise you decided on, review each of the EL #3 points that follow. Discuss whether each adds needed specificity to your Level Two policy. Remember, policy making at any depth is an exercise in clarifying your board's own values, not one of mimicking a standardized recipe. Examine each of the points for content as well. Some of the content may not apply to your situation.

Policy EL #2a (Treatment of Consumers) states: *With respect to interactions with consumers or those applying to be consumers, the CEO shall not cause or allow conditions, procedures, or decisions that are unsafe, undignified, unnecessarily intrusive, or that fail to provide appropriate confidentiality or privacy.*

This policy may be further defined in a number of ways, thereby creating Level Three policies. Here are some of the further policies developed by several of our clients. Notice that the language remains proscriptive as increasing detail is included. At no point does it wander into prescribing the means, that is, into telling the CEO how to manage.

So, becoming even more restraining than EL #1 and EL #2a, the CEO might be told that, according to Policy EL #3a, the CEO shall not

1. Use application forms that elicit information for which there is no clear necessity.
2. Use methods of collecting, reviewing, transmitting, or storing client information that fail to protect against improper access to the material elicited.
3. Maintain facilities that fail to provide a reasonable level of privacy, both visual and aural.
4. Fail to establish with consumers a clear understanding of what may be expected and what may not be expected from the service offered.
5. Fail to inform consumers of this policy or to provide a griev-

ance process to those who believe they have not been accorded a reasonable interpretation of their rights under this policy.

Now, go over the policy at your newly defined Level Three to see if it makes sense as a whole. Does it sufficiently expand your Level Two policy on the same topic? Remember that what will be binding on your CEO will be the combined effects of all the levels with respect to any given topic.

ASSIGNMENT: Discuss this policy and decide whether it is needed at all (being sure to think of it as including all levels thus far), establishes sufficient control, or needs further definition. Deciding that it is not needed means the board is satisfied for the CEO to be limited only by the broader language of EL #1 and EL #2 with respect to this topic. If this EL #3 policy provides the additional necessary and sufficient control, the CEO will have the right to use any reasonable interpretation of its narrower language. If still greater control of CEO options is needed, consider language even more detailed as you go on your own into Level Four policies or beyond.

Policy EL #2b (Treatment of Staff) states: *With respect to the treatment of paid and volunteer staff, the CEO may not cause or allow conditions that are unfair or undignified.* Further definition will create Level Three policies by defining what is meant by the words *unfair* and *undignified* and might even make differentiations between paid and volunteer staff. Notice that the language remains proscriptive as increasing detail is included. At no point does it prescribe means.

Even more restraining than EL #1 and EL #2b would be to tell the CEO that, according to Policy EL #3b, the CEO shall not

1. Operate without written personnel policies that clarify personnel rules for staff, provide for effective handling of grievances, and protect against wrongful conditions such as nepotism and grossly preferential treatment for personal reasons.
2. Discriminate against any staff member for expressing an ethical dissent.

3. Prevent staff from grieving to the board when (1) internal procedures have been exhausted, and (2) the employee alleges either that (3) board policy has been violated to his or her detriment or (4) board policy does not adequately protect his or her human rights.
4. Fail to acquaint staff with their rights under this policy.

In EL #3b, Section 3, we are not intending to imply that boards should necessarily involve themselves in staff grievances. Many boards do not do so and would omit this provision. If your board decides to be involved in staff grievances, the wording outlines a way for them to ensure that the CEO does not prevent them from hearing complaints *about their policies*. This allows boards to avoid second guessing CEO decisions in the delegated area.

It is common for boards to worry about the monitoring of this policy. We advise, as always, that monitoring methods be considered separately from setting the criteria. Monitoring will be discussed in Chapter Six when we deal with Board-CEO Linkage policies.

ASSIGNMENT: Discuss this policy and decide whether it is needed at all (being sure to think of it as including all levels thus far), establishes sufficient control, or needs further definition. Deciding that it is not needed means the board is satisfied for the CEO to be limited only by the broader language of EL #1 and EL #2 with respect to this topic. If this EL #3 policy provides the additional necessary and sufficient control, the CEO will have the right to use any reasonable interpretation of its narrower language. If still greater control of CEO options is needed, consider language even more detailed as you go on your own into Level Four policies or beyond.

Policy EL #2c (Financial Planning and Budgeting) states: *Financial planning for any fiscal year or the remaining part of any fiscal year shall not deviate materially from the board's Ends priorities, risk fiscal jeopardy, or fail to be derived from a multiyear plan.* A policy developed like EL #2c, combined with the greater detail afforded by EL #3c, enables a board to establish more control before telling its CEO that *any* budget that does not violate its values as expressed in policy is acceptable.

Even more restraining than EL #1 and EL #2c would be to tell the CEO that, according to Policy EL #3c, the CEO shall not allow budgeting that

1. Contains too little information to enable credible projection of revenues and expenses, separation of capital and operational items, cash flow, and disclosure of planning assumptions.
2. Plans the expenditure in any fiscal year of more funds than are conservatively projected to be received in that period.
3. Reduces the current assets at any time to less than twice current liabilities [or allows cash to drop below a safety reserve of less than $_____ at any time].
4. Provides less for board prerogatives during the year than is set forth in the Cost of Governance policy.

Notice that each statement is a further defined criterion about budgeting. At no point does the policy say anything about board approval. Board approval is not a criterion about the nature of budgeting. It is merely an action that implies the board is afraid its criteria setting is insufficient, therefore it wants to take another look at any budget or budget change, using whatever criteria come to mind at that time.

Pay particular attention, as always, to those words upon which CEO interpretation might cause the board the most worry. For example, what is *conservative* projection? The term surely has meaning, but is its range of meaning acceptable? Notice, too, that the requirement for cash flow to be an integral part of the CEO's planning is more stringent than most nonprofit and public boards have typically been. Notice that the board takes responsibility for clarifying what it will spend on governance and instructs the CEO to put that amount aside for the board.

ASSIGNMENT: Discuss this policy and decide whether it is needed at all (being sure to think of it as including all levels thus far), establishes sufficient control, or needs further definition. Deciding that it is not needed means the board is satisfied for the CEO to be limited only by the broader language of EL #1 and EL #2 with respect to this topic. If this EL #3 policy provides the additional necessary and sufficient control, the CEO will have the right to use any reasonable interpretation of its narrower language. If still greater control of CEO options is needed, consider language even more detailed as you go on your own into Level Four policies or beyond.

Policy EL #2d (Financial Condition and Activities) states: *With respect to the actual, ongoing financial condition and activities, the CEO shall not cause or allow the development of fiscal jeopardy or a material deviation of actual expenditures from board priorities established in Ends policies.* Even more restraining than EL #1 and EL #2d would be to tell the CEO that, according to Policy EL #3d, the CEO shall not

1. Expend more funds than have been received in the fiscal year to date unless the debt guideline (to follow) is met.
2. Indebt the organization in an amount greater than can be repaid by certain, otherwise unencumbered revenues within sixty days.
3. Use any long-term reserves.
4. Conduct interfund shifting in amounts greater than can be restored to a condition of discrete fund balances by certain, otherwise unencumbered revenue within thirty days.
5. Fail to settle payroll and debts in a timely manner.
6. Allow tax payments or other government-ordered payments or filings to be overdue or inaccurately filed.
7. Make a single purchase or commitment of greater than $_____.
8. Acquire, encumber, or dispose of real property.
9. Fail to aggressively pursue receivables after a reasonable grace period.

EL #3d shows how, if it wishes, a board may place certain operations completely off-limits to the CEO (Sections 3 and 8). Remember, though, that an item taken out of the CEO's authority would have to become part of the board's own hands-on responsibility. Section 4 only makes sense when there is fund accounting, not in every organization.

Section 7 demonstrates a method of placing a spending limit on the CEO. Such a limit would require that the board make spending decisions in excess of the sum named. Traditional boards commonly place ridiculously low limits on the CEO. Policy Governance boards commonly find that their concerns are so well covered by policy that they can be far more liberal in the spending ability they give to the CEO, sometimes to the point of imposing no limit at all. We are not, by including Section 7, implying that the board should necessarily set a spending limit on single purchases.

Now, go over the policy at your newly defined Level Three to see if it makes sense as a whole. Does it sufficiently expand your Level Two policy on the same topic?

ASSIGNMENT: Discuss this policy and decide whether it is needed at all (being sure to think of it as including all levels thus far), establishes sufficient control, or needs further definition. Deciding that it is not needed means the board is satisfied for the CEO to be limited only by the broader language of EL #1 and EL #2 with respect to this topic. If this EL #3 policy provides the additional necessary and sufficient control, the CEO will have the right to use any reasonable interpretation of its narrower language. If still greater control of CEO options is needed, consider language even more detailed as you go on your own into Level Four policies or beyond.

Policy EL #2e (Emergency CEO Succession) states: *In order to protect the board from sudden loss of CEO services, the CEO may have no fewer than two other executives familiar with board and CEO issues and processes.* We have no EL #3 statements to suggest for this policy. It is the only EL #2-level statement for which neither of the authors has ever had a client who went into more detail. If you want to do so, consider expanding upon the interpretation of *familiar* and perhaps upon which *issues* and *processes* are meant.

ASSIGNMENT: You have already discussed whether this policy can stand alone (during your work on Level Two). Regardless of what we have usually found, does your board wish to go into further definitions at Level Three? If so, do so at this time.

Policy EL #2f (Asset Protection) states: *The CEO shall not allow the assets to be unprotected, inadequately maintained, or unnecessarily risked.* If you need to be more restraining in definition than EL #1 and EL #2f, the CEO might be told that, according to Policy EL #3f, the CEO shall not

1. Fail to insure against theft and casualty losses to at least 80 percent of replacement value and against liability losses to board members, staff, and the organization itself in an amount greater than the average for comparable organizations.
2. Allow unbonded personnel access to material amounts of funds.
3. Subject plant and equipment to improper wear and tear or insufficient maintenance.
4. Unnecessarily expose the organization, its board, or its staff to claims of liability.
5. Make any purchase (1) wherein normally prudent protection has not been given against conflict of interest; (2) of over $_____ without having obtained comparative prices and quality; (3) of over $_____ without a stringent method of assuring the balance of long-term quality and cost.
6. Fail to protect intellectual property, information, and files from loss or significant damage.
7. Receive, process, or disburse funds under controls that are insufficient to meet the board-appointed auditor's standards.
8. Invest or hold operating capital in insecure instruments, including uninsured checking accounts and bonds of less than AA rating, or in non-interest bearing accounts except when necessary to facilitate ease in operational transactions.
9. Endanger the organization's public image or credibility, particularly in ways that would hinder its accomplishment of mission.

Is 80 percent of replacement value the right amount? Do you need to specify it at all? Should you use a fixed rather than comparative amount for liability coverage? Are the three different levels of care in purchasing needed or simply superfluous? Does it make sense to think of public image as an asset? Are the investment criteria in Section 8 appropriate for your organization? These and other issues beg for discussion.

ASSIGNMENT: Discuss this policy and decide whether it is needed at all (being sure to think of it as including all levels thus far), es-

EXECUTIVE LIMITATIONS POLICIES

tablishes sufficient control, or needs further definition. Deciding that it is not needed means the board is satisfied for the CEO to be limited only by the broader language of EL #1 and EL #2 with respect to this topic. If this EL #3 policy provides the additional necessary and sufficient control, the CEO will have the right to use any reasonable interpretation of its narrower language. If still greater control of CEO options is needed, consider language even more detailed as you go on your own into Level Four policies or beyond.

Policy EL#2g (Compensation and Benefits) states: *With respect to employment, compensation, and benefits to employees, consultants, contract workers, and volunteers, the CEO shall not cause or allow jeopardy to fiscal integrity or public image.*

This policy as well may be further defined, perhaps by EL #3g language like the following. Even more restraining than EL #1 and EL #2g would be to tell the CEO that, according to Policy EL #3g (Level Four is reached in Section 5), the CEO shall not

1. Change his or her own compensation and benefits.
2. Promise or imply permanent or guaranteed employment.
3. Establish current compensation and benefits that deviate materially from the geographic or professional market for the skills employed.
4. Create compensation obligations over a longer term than revenues can be safely projected, in no event longer than one year and in all events subject to losses in revenue.
5. Establish or change pension benefits so as to cause unpredictable or inequitable situations.
   a. Incur unfunded liabilities.
   b. Provide less than some basic level of benefits to all full-time employees, though differential benefits to encourage longevity are not prohibited.
   c. Allow any employee to lose benefits already accrued from any foregoing plan.
   d. Treat the CEO differently from other key employees.

Your board will doubtlessly have to argue some of the foregoing points. To illustrate, the CEO's authority to make changes in pension plans is curtailed in three steps: (1) by the initial provisions of EL #1, (2) by the more specific provisions of EL #2g (and any other relevant policies, for example, financial condition and staff treatment), and now (3) by Sections 5a through 5d of this policy. You might need to use a pension consultant to help you with these provisions, but be sure the consultant understands the Policy Governance approach to board control of these matters. If your board wants the CEO to have no authority over pensions, you would merely reduce Section 5 to its first five words, "Establish or change pension benefits," deleting the remainder of Section 5 *and its lettered subparts.* That will take pension determinations out of the CEO's hands entirely. But the board must then be willing to be responsible for the matter, and that will likely require the same degree of study of the principles involved.

ASSIGNMENT: Discuss this policy and decide whether it is needed at all (being sure to think of it as including all levels thus far), establishes sufficient control, or needs further definition. Deciding that it is not needed means the board is satisfied for the CEO to be limited only by the broader language of EL #1 and EL #2 with respect to this topic. If this EL #3 policy provides the additional necessary and sufficient control, the CEO will have the right to use any reasonable interpretation of its narrower language. If still greater control of CEO options is needed, consider language even more detailed as you go on your own into Level Four policies or beyond.

Policy EL #2h (Communication and Support to the Board) states: *The CEO shall not permit the board to be uninformed or unsupported in its work.* To further restrict the range of CEO interpretations of EL #1 and EL #2h, the board might add that, according to Policy EL #3h, the CEO shall not

1. Neglect to submit monitoring data required by the board (see policy on Monitoring Executive Performance) in a timely, accurate, and understandable fashion, directly addressing provisions of board policies being monitored.
2. Let the board be unaware of relevant trends, anticipated adverse media coverage, and material external and internal

changes, particularly changes in the assumptions upon which any board policy has previously been established.

3. Fail to advise the board if, in the CEO's opinion, the board is not in compliance with its own policies on Governance Process and Board-CEO Linkage, particularly in the case of board behavior that is detrimental to the work relationship between the board and the CEO.

4. Fail to marshal for the board as many staff and external points of view, issues, and options as needed for fully informed board choices.

5. Present information in unnecessarily complex or lengthy form or in a form that fails to differentiate among information of three types: monitoring, decision preparation, and other.

6. Fail to provide a mechanism for official board, officer, or committee communications.

7. Fail to deal with the board as a whole except when fulfilling individual requests for information or responding to officers or committees duly charged by the board.

8. Fail to report in a timely manner an actual or anticipated noncompliance with any policy of the board.

9. Fail to supply for the consent agenda all items delegated to the CEO, yet required by law or contract to be board-approved, along with the monitoring assurance pertaining thereto.

Policy Governance requires boards to understand the difference between what they wish to control and what they *simply wish to know about*. In addition to the sharing of certain monitoring data, quickly dispensed with in Section 1, this policy allows the board to say what it wishes to be informed about, things about which it has set no criteria. It is important to remember that the board can form no judgments of CEO performance from these no-criteria items, but the board will be informed about them.

The board can, of course, later set criteria on these matters, after which the topics "graduate" to monitorable items, not just ones to satisfy board curiosity. Since many boards feel that they know only what the CEO decides to tell them, this policy is useful in removing from the CEO the need either to guess about or to manipulate what the board wants. Section 2 can provide a useful listing of desired incidental information. Does the list include all the information the board wants? The CEO can, of course, give the board whatever additional information he or she chooses, but the CEO cannot omit the items listed by the board.

ASSIGNMENT: Discuss this policy and decide whether it is needed at all (being sure to think of it as including all levels thus far), establishes sufficient control, or needs further definition. Deciding that it is not needed means the board is satisfied for the CEO to be limited only by the broader language of EL #1 and EL #2 with respect to this topic. If this EL #3 policy provides the additional necessary and sufficient control, the CEO will have the right to use any reasonable interpretation of its narrower language. If still greater control of CEO options is needed, consider language even more detailed as you go on your own into Level Four policies or beyond.

Policy EL #2i (Ends Focus of Grants or Contracts) states: *The CEO may not enter into any grant or contract arrangements that fail to emphasize primarily the production of Ends and, secondarily, the avoidance of unacceptable means.* Remember our note earlier that this sample is included to illustrate an atypical policy, one that applies only to grant-making or subcontracting organizations. If it does not apply to your organization as do the previous generic issues, please skip past it.

This policy clarifies that the purpose of funding or contracting with organizations is to purchase certain results for certain recipients at the cost being granted. The CEO is required to make this the primary consideration in decisions regarding funding. In order to further restrict the range of possible CEO interpretations of statements already found in EL #1 and EL #2h, the board may add that, according to Policy EL #3i, the CEO shall not

1. Fail to prohibit particular methods and activities to preclude grant funds from being used in imprudent, unlawful, or unethical ways.
2. Fail to assess and consider an applicant's capability to produce appropriately targeted, efficient results.
3. Fund specific methods except when doing so for research purposes, when the result to be achieved is knowledge about differential effectiveness of various methods.

Does your board find these additional three EL #3i points necessary, or are they covered quite well enough by the EL #2i statement? It is certainly important that your CEO is held accountable for Ends and Executive Limitations, regardless of whether the achievements and behaviors are in-house or contracted out. Note that Section 3 has the effect of leaving an opening for a very specific kind of attention to means.

ASSIGNMENT: Discuss this policy and decide whether it is needed at all (being sure to think of it as including all levels thus far), establishes sufficient control, or needs further definition. Deciding that it is not needed means the board is satisfied for the CEO to be limited only by the broader language of EL #1 and EL #2 with respect to this topic. If this EL #3 policy provides the additional necessary and sufficient control, the CEO will have the right to use any reasonable interpretation of its narrower language. If still greater control of CEO options is needed, consider language even more detailed as you go on your own into Level Four policies or beyond.

Let's Check the Map to See Where We Are

You now have a policy quadrant that your board, depending on your decisions in the foregoing exercise, has controlled all the way to Level Three, at least on some topics. This has been the most common depth for our clients to reach before delegating to the CEO. But it need not be the level at which your board delegates any particular issue. Let us illustrate in Figure 4.4 what the policy making will have done so far if your board is similar to most of our client boards.

Remember the pairing of two important rules. First, the board has the choice of further defining any policy provision it enacts. Second, the board has the obligation to allow the CEO to use any reasonable interpretation of whatever language the board decides is sufficient. Monitoring CEO performance will be against the policy language the board *chose*, not the language it *meant*. When we refer to monitoring always being against criteria, the criteria we mean are the words (and sometimes numbers) of the policies. In short, the policies *are* the monitoring criteria. All the CEO will have to do is convince the board that he or she has attained or avoided a reasonable interpretation of those words.

Figure 4.4. Executive Limitations Policies Completed.

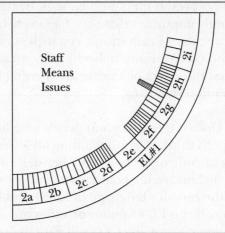

Note: Your Executive Limitations policies cover all possibilities (because they begin at the broadest level) yet extend to the board-desired level of specificity. Now it is safe to say, with respect to operational means, if the board has not said no, the answer is yes!

   In order to address the creation of Executive Limitations policies, we have had to assume that the board has made the decision to delegate in the Policy Governance manner. Of course, you would not be using this book if you hadn't decided to follow Policy Governance concepts, so we feel safe in the assumption. The assumption is made explicit in Chapter Six where we demonstrate the manner in which Policy Governance boards delegate authority into the operating organization, define the job of the CEO, and monitor the appropriate use of the delegated authority.

Next Chapter

Next we turn in Chapter Five to developing the Governance Process policies, ones in which the board determines the features of its own job. In this category of policies, the Policy Governance board establishes its own tailored statements committing it to proper governance.

Governance Process Policies
Defining the Board's Job

In this chapter we focus on those policies with which the board instructs itself and subparts of itself, such as officers and committees, about its own job. This category, Governance Process, appears on the circle diagram first presented in Chapter Two in the upper left-hand quadrant and as shown in Figure 5.1. Of course, there are other legitimate titles that could be used for this policy category, such as Board Job.

It is in this quadrant that the board explicitly describes the standards of group and individual behavior to which it agrees to hold itself. Remarkably, it is unusual for traditional boards to discuss or decide issues that are routinely addressed by the Governance Process policies that you will find in this chapter. We think your board will find the exercise of making explicit rules challenging and rewarding. Having a succinct description of the board's job and the manner in which it will operate is not only handy for new board members but useful as a continuing guide to experienced ones as well. But more important, having a carefully thought out process for governing will go nowhere unless it is codified. Under Policy Governance this self-examination is a required exercise. The process by which a group fulfills its governing commitment will not occur in a defensible form by chance.

We are more directive in this chapter and in Chapter Six in terms of the levels of policy your board goes into because these two chapters deal with describing the board's own means. Our reason is not that the policies need greater depth in order to work, because the chairperson will be given the right to flesh them out with

Figure 5.1. The Governance Process Quadrant.

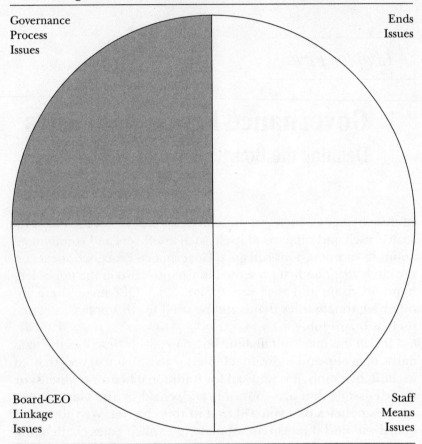

Governance
Process
Issues

Ends
Issues

Board-CEO
Linkage
Issues

Staff
Means
Issues

Note: On the circle diagram introduced in Chapter Two, the issues dealt with in this chapter are in the upper left-hand quadrant.

his or her interpretation. Our reason is that in most cases *the board needs the personal buy-in and understanding that comes from developing the greater depth.*

But there is another reason for in-depth attention to Governance Process and Board-CEO Linkage policies, regardless of the board's philosophy about policy depth in Ends and Executive Limitations. Although Policy Governance is a conceptual model that appears in the authors' books and other publications, *your board's model of governance can only be found in its Governance Process and*

Board-CEO Linkage policies. In other words, these two categories of board means policies *are* the governance model for you. For that reason, it will serve you and your subsequent replacements well to have a relatively thorough description of your plan of governance.

As we begin, then, remember that as in the other policy categories, policy development proceeds from the most general and inclusive level to levels of further specificity. An orderly sequence is used, and the board stops defining its words when it can accept any reasonable interpretation by the chair.

Let's Take It from the Top: Level One

The most general and inclusive policy—the largest-mixing-bowl policy—used by most of our clients relies on language similar to the following:

Policy GP #1: Global Governance Process Policy

The purpose of the board, on behalf of [identify the ownership here], is to see to it that [name of organization] (1) achieves what it should and (2) avoids unacceptable actions and situations.

You will notice that the statement, broad as it is, incorporates the key concepts that the board acts upon on behalf of a larger group and that it must assure accountable organizational performance. It introduces the concept of separating required ends from unacceptable means, and most important, makes the point that the board must ensure the accomplishment of what it has decided the organization must attain. This policy declares the board's leadership duty in an unmistakable fashion. In a sense, it starkly states the reason for having a board at all, so there is no place to hide.

The policy requires the board to identify its ownership. This may be no easy task. In membership organizations, the membership is almost certainly the ownership. In city councils, the citizens are the owners. Our community-based clients often eventually decide that it is the community itself whose interest must be expressed by the board. But many organizations (for example, a public radio station) will find the ownership not nearly as easy to name. It is tempting for boards to take a shortcut and act as if they represent the consumers, the staff, or the funders. But while these may be *part* of the total ownership, they are not owners by virtue of these roles.

Globally addressing the role of governance in the organization is, like all Level One policies, necessarily broad and open to a wide range of interpretation. Policy Governance as a complete model, of course, places the right to interpret Governance Process policies primarily in the hands of the board chairperson and, secondarily, anyone else to whom the board explicitly delegates. As this chapter progresses, we get to the policy in which the board explicitly grants the chair the right to interpret policy language in both Governance Process and Board-CEO Linkage categories.

We assume that you will follow our sequence as it leads toward giving the chairperson the right and obligation to interpret and implement board wishes as expressed in these policies. That assumption allows us to remind you of the reasonable interpretation test at each stage, even before we have taken you to the point where there is anyone to reasonably interpret!

ASSIGNMENT: Discuss the wording of this Level One Governance Process policy, arriving at wording that both expresses your board's global intent for governance and, at the same time, is model-consistent with Policy Governance principles. After arriving at your final wording, you are ready to proceed into the more detailed wording that we recommend.

At this stage, with Governance Process Level One in place, the policy coverage is visually presented in Figure 5.2.

Here's a Little More Detail: Going to Level Two

You may not be surprised to know that we have never seen a board leave further interpretation to its chair at this stage. Faced with having to further define their expectations in Governance Process, most boards have found that their more detailed policy making falls into the following Level Two topic areas:

- Governing style (the way in which the board goes about its task)
- Board job description (what the board is to produce; job outputs)

Figure 5.2. Governance Process, Level One.

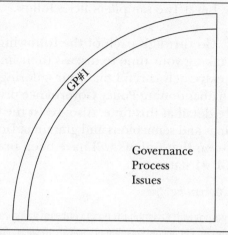

Governance
Process
Issues

Note: In the Governance Process quadrant of the policy circle, GP #1 encloses all further considerations.

- Chairperson's role (apportioning some of the board's authority to the chair)
- Board members' code of conduct (what is expected of individual members)
- Board committee principles (philosophy and rules about using committees)
- Cost of governance (putting a value on board capability and contribution)

    This chapter will guide you through these policy topics, as well as policy topics found at more detailed levels, should your board wish to pursue the greater detail. Policies dealing with the topics just listed will be referred to as *GP #2 policies.* To keep them separate, we'll attach a letter suffix to each. Accordingly, the policy entitled Governing Style will be referred to as GP #2a, and the others will follow suit.

    Remember that the policy wording shown may not be the exact words your board should use. But the language we present demonstrates the manner of developing policies in this quadrant that are consistent with Policy Governance. If your board decides to use the samples, it will doubtless need to adapt the wording to match its own values. The Level Two sample policies follow.

ASSIGNMENT: Go through each of the following GP #2 statements in turn, taking your time to discuss their implications for your board. Be extremely careful that your tailoring of these policies not result in abandoning Policy Governance principles. Resist going into more detail at this time. Also, resist the temptation to word-craft commas and semicolons and grammar. Don't forget that each consideration that follows will have been preceded by the more general GP #1 statement.

Policy GP #2a: Governing Style

The board will govern with an emphasis on (1) outward vision rather than internal preoccupation, (2) encouragement of diversity in viewpoints, (3) strategic leadership more than administrative detail, (4) clear distinction of board and chief executive roles, (5) collective rather than individual decisions, (6) future rather than past or present, and (7) proactivity rather than reactivity.

At first reading, you may be tempted to dismiss this policy as motherhood and apple pie. After all, who can argue with it? But please note that it commits the board to a style that is rarely seen in governing boards. Of course, the policy is quite general, as would be expected at Level Two, but it establishes a required board behavior capable of accomplishing the obligation set out in GP #1.

Note that the language does not prevent the board from involving itself in current issues, short-term issues, internal matters, or even in being reactive. It merely pledges the board to govern *with an emphasis* on the more profound end of the spectrum.

ASSIGNMENT: Discuss the implications of this policy for your board. Keep in mind that you will judge board conduct against these provisions in the future, so these words are not merely window dressing. We always recommend that boards further define this policy and encourage you to examine the Level Three policy that is presented later in this chapter.

Policy GP #2b: Board Job Description

The specific job outputs of the board are those unique "values-added" that tie ownership prerogatives to organizational performance.

This policy introduces the obligation of specifiable job products peculiar to the board itself, as distinct from outputs of the organization. The board is here committing itself to produce whatever outputs will connect those who own the organization to the performance of the organization. Our clients always go to a Level Three policy to more exactly define these products, which consist of those outputs generic to governance anywhere plus any additional ones chosen by a specific board. A third level of this policy will be shown later in the chapter.

ASSIGNMENT: Discuss the implications of this policy for your board. Keep in mind that you will judge board conduct against these provisions in the future, so these words are not merely window dressing. We always recommend that boards further define this policy and encourage you to examine the Level Three policy that is presented later in this chapter.

Policy GP #2c: Chairperson's Role

The chairperson assures the integrity and fulfillment of the board's process and, secondarily, occasionally represents the board to outside parties.

Notice that this policy moves us from defining the role of the board to defining that of the chair or, more accurately, by describing the value-added created by the chair. We use this policy and its secondary reference to the chair "occasionally" speaking to outside parties as a reminder that the chair's role is intimately related to the board's job, not to the CEO's. Note that the job of assuring fulfillment of the board's process sets the foundation for, and could be said to be the broad statement of, delegation of a specific right to interpret the board's words as far as the board's own process is concerned.

ASSIGNMENT: Discuss the implications of this policy for your board. Keep in mind not only that you will judge the chair's conduct against this policy in the future, but also that these words grant authority to the chair. We always recommend that boards further define this policy and encourage you to examine the Level Three policy that is presented later in this chapter.

Policy GP #2d: Board Member's Code of Conduct

The board commits itself and its members to ethical, businesslike, and lawful
conduct, including proper use of authority and appropriate decorum when
acting as board members.

Having dealt with the board's job and the chair's job, policy development in the Governance Process category turns to the definition of the expectations placed on individual board members. If your board already has a code of conduct, it may be that it can be placed into this category as it is. Check it, though, to ensure that it places demands or restrictions on board members that are required by Policy Governance. This short statement goes beyond the usual conflict of interest provisions.

ASSIGNMENT: Discuss the implications of this policy for your board. Keep in mind that you will judge board member conduct against these provisions in the future, so these words are not merely window dressing. We always recommend that boards further define this policy and encourage you to examine the Level Three policy that is presented later in this chapter.

Policy GP #2e: Board Committee Principles

Board committees, when used, will be assigned so as to reinforce the wholeness
of the board's job and so as never to interfere with delegation from board to
CEO.

It is useful to recall the definition of committees. A board committee is any group of people that is set up by, instructed by, and ordered to report to the board, no matter who is in the group or what the group is called. Even as broadly stated as this policy is, it is clear that under Policy Governance many traditionally sanctioned committees would not belong to the board, if they existed at all. This is because many traditional committees do interfere with delegation from board to CEO. Our clients find this principle easy to understand. If they experience difficulty with it, the difficulty usually surrounds the political awkwardness of disbanding an established committee.

ASSIGNMENT: Discuss the implications of this policy for your board. Keep in mind that you will judge future board actions with respect to committees against these provisions. We always recommend that boards further define this policy and encourage you to examine the Level Three policy that is presented later in this chapter.

Policy GP #2f: Cost of Governance

Because poor governance costs more than learning to govern well, the board will invest in its governance capacity.

Boards seldom recognize the costs that they themselves incur, though they are more aware of their direct costs than of others. Direct costs include meeting and travel expense, though these are usually the smaller, if more visible, costs of governance. Larger costs include the expense of staff time in servicing unnecessary board committees or producing unnecessary reports. The greatest expense of governance, however, is in the waste that results from organizational resources being expended in the absence of any required Ends. This policy is cognizant of all of these costs and maintains that the cost of even minor lack of capability is likely to be greater than the cost of education.

ASSIGNMENT: Discuss the implications of this policy for your board. Keep in mind that you will judge board conduct against these provisions in the future. We always recommend that boards further define this policy and encourage you to examine the Level Three policy that is presented later in this chapter.

Let's Check the Map to See Where We Are

The Level Two policies listed earlier further define the broadest Governance Process policy, GP #1. They are shown in Figure 5.3 as having clarified the initial policy, and as having narrowed the range of possible interpretation of that policy.

Going into Even More Detail: Level Three

A third level of policy development would further define expectations the board has of itself. It simultaneously outlines the rules

Figure 5.3. Governance Process, Levels One and Two.

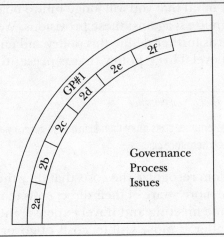

Governance
Process
Issues

Note: More depth, that is, definition, has been added by GP #2 policies in the Governance Process quadrant, leaving less decision latitude to the chair.

that the board will ask its chair to further define and enforce. Since the effect is to leave the chair less range of interpretation, a third level provides greater specificity as to the intentions of the board as a whole.

In the following pages, we demonstrate some Level Three policies. Once again, we remind you that we do recommend this level of specificity. We return to the policies you just completed and take their provisions into more detail.

ASSIGNMENT: For each of the GP #2 policies in the previous exercise, review each of the GP #3 points that follow, considering their implications for your board. Be extremely careful that if you tailor these policies, you do not abandon Policy Governance principles. Don't forget that each consideration that follows will have been preceded by the more general GP #1 and GP #2 statements.

Governing Style

Policy GP #2a states: *The board will govern with an emphasis on (1) outward vision rather than internal preoccupation, (2) encouragement of di-*

versity in viewpoints, (3) strategic leadership more than administrative detail, (4) clear distinction of board and chief executive roles, (5) collective rather than individual decisions, (6) future rather than past or present, and (7) proactivity rather than reactivity. While this policy includes a great deal already, our clients have found that expanding its implications for board operating style is instructive. Your Level Three policy, then, might be as follows:

GP #3a   Governing Style: Level Three

1. The board will cultivate a sense of group responsibility. The board, not the staff, will be responsible for excellence in governing. The board will be the initiator of policy, not merely a reactor to staff initiatives. The board will use the expertise of individual members to enhance the ability of the board as a body rather than to substitute individual judgments for the board's values. The board will allow no officer, individual, or committee of the board to hinder or be an excuse for not fulfilling board commitments.

2. The board will direct, control, and inspire the organization through the careful establishment of broad written policies reflecting the board's values and perspectives about ends to be achieved and means to be avoided. The board's major policy focus will be on the intended long-term effects outside the organization, not on the administrative or programmatic means of attaining those effects.

3. The board will enforce upon itself whatever discipline is needed to govern with excellence. Discipline will apply to matters such as attendance, preparation, policy-making principles, respect of roles, and ensuring continuance of governance capability. Continual board development will include orientation of new board members in the board's governance process and periodic board discussion of process improvement.

4. The board will monitor and discuss the board's process and performance at each meeting. Self-monitoring will include comparison of board activity and discipline to policies in the Governance Process and Board-CEO Linkage categories.

Look over the combination of commitments now set into place by Level One, Two, and Three policies. Are they descriptive of the kind of board process to which your board would commit? Is a further level required in any area? Our clients usually notice at this point that their current attendance requirement is merely for courtesy (phoning in so an absence can be counted as "excused") rather than for ensuring that people show up. In any event, the governance commitment signaled by this policy is greater than many boards have previously taken on. Discuss the implications fully.

Your board may also wish to expand upon the method to be used for board orientation or for board self-evaluation. If it does, then a subsection can be added to the appropriate point, thereby taking this policy into Level Four.

Some boards express surprise that the policy we offer requires board self-evaluation on a meeting-by-meeting basis. We ask boards to consider that self-evaluation is a way to ensure that the board stays on track with its new governance style. Since it is so easy to stray from new territory into familiar territory, frequent self-evaluation is called for. In fact, we expect any board that self-evaluates less often will have a hard time keeping integrity in its governing task.

ASSIGNMENT: Discuss and decide whether the parts of this Level Three policy can stand alone (being sure to think of any policy as including all levels thus far) or needs further definition. If you desire more definition than is provided in Level Three, consider language even more detailed as you go on your own into Level Four policies or beyond.

Board Job Description

Policy GP #2b states: *The specific job outputs of the board are those unique values-added that tie ownership prerogatives to organizational performance.* Building upon GP #2b, it is common for boards to proceed to a Level Three policy in order to articulate the job products to which it refers. We believe this will be useful for your board. Consider the following as a Level Three policy (this sample contains elements of Level Four as well). Remember that the language is an expansion of the meaning of job outputs or values-added that bind ownership to performance. The way we do this is to posit an output style job description rather than an activity style description. In other words, the point is not what the board stays busy doing but what it produces. That is why the language that follows is not the more familiar list of activities we are accustomed to in job descriptions.

GP #3b   Board Job Description: Level Three

1. The board will produce the link between the organization and the ownership.

2. The board will produce written governing policies that, at the broadest levels, address each category of organizational decision.

    a. Ends: Organizational products, effects, benefits, outcomes, recipients, and their cost or relative worth (what good for which recipients at what cost).

    b. Executive Limitations: Constraints on executive authority that establish the prudence and ethics boundaries within which all executive activity and decisions must take place.

    c. Governance Process: Specification of how the board conceives, carries out, and monitors its own task.

    d. Board-CEO Linkage: How power is delegated and its proper use monitored; authority and accountability of the CEO role.

3. The board will produce assurance of CEO performance (against policies in 2a and 2b).

Now, go over the Level Three policy and see if it sufficiently defines your Level Two policy. In this example, the board is of course listing those products it holds *itself* accountable for producing. Nothing, in other words, that has been delegated to the CEO would show up on this list. Your board may feel that additional items should be added. If your board has placed some organizational assets off-limits to the CEO, the care of those assets would be included in the board's own job description. In addition, your board may hold itself accountable for some aspect of donor funding. The board should be clear about what it is in fact taking on. If it is committed to finding prospective donors, it should say this. If it is committed to selling gala tickets, it should say so. If it is responsible for all aspects of fundraising (this is rarely the case), it should say this. Both the board and the CEO are then clear about who does what.

We encourage boards to consider Level Four and Five policies that expand upon the list of board products into a plan for future agendas. We offer the following Level Four and Five policies for your examination.

Policy GP #4b   Board Job Description: Level Four

To accomplish its job products with a governance style consistent with board policies, the board will follow an annual agenda that (1) completes re-exploration of Ends policies annually and (2) continually improves board performance through board education and enriched input and deliberation.

Policy GP #5b   Board Job Description: Level Five

1. The cycle will conclude each year on the last day of September so that administrative planning and budgeting can be based on accomplishing a one-year segment of the board's most recent statement of long-term Ends.

2. The cycle will start with the board's development of its agenda for the next year.

   a. Consultations with selected groups in the ownership, or other methods of gaining ownership input, will be determined and arranged in the first quarter, to be held during the balance of the year.

   b. Governance education and education related to ends determination (for example, presentations by futurists, demographers, advocacy groups, and staff) will be arranged in the first quarter, to be held during the balance of the year.

3. Throughout the year, the board will attend to consent agenda items as expeditiously as possible.

4. CEO monitoring will be included on the agenda if monitoring reports show policy violations or if policy criteria are to be debated.

5. CEO remuneration will be decided after a review of monitoring reports received in the last year during the month of February.

Notice that using this method, your board can transition from deciding on its job products to arranging its agenda around their accomplishment. This enables the board to be in control of its own agenda. Your board will perhaps wish to establish an even more detailed policy about annual planning. The rule is, as always, that the board should define its words in enough detail that any reasonable interpretation by the chair would be acceptable. With a policy like the foregoing sample and armed with the authority to use any reasonable interpretation, any chair would be able to arrange the fine tuning of agendas. The board agenda can truly become the board's agenda, not the CEO's agenda for the board.

ASSIGNMENT: Discuss and decide whether the parts of these Level Three, Four, and Five policies can stand alone (being sure to think of any policy as including all levels thus far), or need further definition. If you desire more definition than provided in the levels shown, consider language even more detailed as you go on your own into further levels.

Chairperson's Role

Policy GP #2c states: *The chairperson assures the integrity and fulfill- ment of the board's process and, secondarily, occasionally represents the board to outside parties.* Your chair has an important role in ensuring that the board stays on track and abides by its own rules. While every member of the board has a responsibility to exercise disci- pline in the group, the chair has a special role in this respect. For this reason, many of our clients decide in favor of including a third and fourth policy level regarding the chair's role. We strongly en- courage you to do the same. In the following policy, GP #3c, we have shown a fourth level of detail.

GP #3c   Chairperson's Role: Levels Three and Four

1. The job result of the chairperson is that the board behaves consistently with its own rules and those legitimately imposed upon it from outside the organization.

    a. Meeting discussion content will be only issues that, according to board policy, clearly belong to the board to decide, not the CEO.

    b. Deliberation will be fair, open, and thorough but also timely, orderly, and to the point.

2. The authority of the chairperson consists in making decisions that fall within topics covered by board policies on Governance Process and Board-CEO Linkage, except where the board specifically delegates por- tions of this authority to others. The chairperson is authorized to use any reasonable interpretation of the provisions in these policies.

a. The chairperson is empowered to chair board meetings with all the commonly accepted power of that position (for example, ruling, recognizing).

b. The chairperson has no authority to make decisions about policies created by the board within Ends and Executive Limitations policy areas. Therefore, the chairperson has no authority to supervise or direct the CEO.

c. The chairperson may represent the board to outside parties in announcing board-stated positions and in stating chair decisions and interpretations within the area delegated to her or him.

d. The chairperson may delegate this authority but remains accountable for its use.

You will notice that this policy at Level Three divides the chairperson's job into its output performance and its authority. In both areas, our Level Four gives further definition to the language. The policy clarifies the powers made available to the chair, as well as those *not* available to this officer.

If you are accustomed to traditional job descriptions, you will be tempted to describe the chair's job in activity rather than outcome terms. Resist the temptation. Just as we stated about the board's job, any position exists to provide specific values-added, not to stay busy at even commendable pursuits.

ASSIGNMENT: Discuss and decide whether the parts of this Level Three and Four policy can stand alone (being sure to think of any policy as including all levels thus far) or needs further definition. If you desire more definition than provided in the levels shown, consider language even more detailed as you go on your own into further levels.

Board Members' Code of Conduct

Policy EL #2d states: *The board commits itself and its members to ethical, businesslike, and lawful conduct, including proper use of authority and appropriate decorum when acting as board members.* Boards vary a great deal in how much further they wish to define their own expected conduct. We suggest going further than this GP #2d policy simply because the new discipline required for Policy Governance calls for board members not only to be very clear about their standards of conduct, which could be defined by the chairperson in his or her interpretation, but take a direct hand in them. Accordingly, we show Level Three and Level Four detail of the policy.

Policy GP #3d   Board Member's Code of Conduct: Levels Three and Four

1. Members must represent unconflicted loyalty to the interests of the ownership. This accountability supersedes any conflicting loyalty such as that to advocacy or interest groups and membership on other boards or staffs. It also supersedes the personal interest of any board member acting as a consumer of the organization's services.

2. Members must avoid conflict of interest with respect to their fiduciary responsibility.

    a. There must be no self-dealing or any conduct of private business or personal services between any board member and the organization, except as procedurally controlled, to assure openness, competitive opportunity, and equal access to inside information.

    b. When the board is to decide upon an issue about which a member has an unavoidable conflict of interest, that member shall absent herself or himself without comment from not only the vote but also from the deliberation.

    c. Board members must not use their positions to obtain employment for themselves, family members, or close associates. Should a member desire employment, he or she must first resign.

    d. Members will annually disclose their involvements with other organizations, with vendors, or any other associations that might produce a conflict.

3. Board members may not attempt to exercise individual authority over the organization except as explicitly set forth in board policies.

    a. Members' interaction with public, press, or other entities must recognize the same limitation and the inability of any board member to speak for the board except to repeat explicitly stated board decisions.

    b. Members will give no consequence or voice to individual judgments of CEO or staff performance.

4. Members will respect the confidentiality appropriate to issues of a sensitive nature.

Some boards find this a difficult policy to decide upon. It so explicitly limits the power of individuals and sets out expectations for their conduct that it may seem to seriously challenge some of the freedom sometimes assumed by board members. This is one requirement we are totally unapologetic about. Governance is too important to be compromised by individual board members' needs or wants.

You may wish to discuss the special mention made of loyalty to subparts of the ownership, especially our suggestion about consumers on the board. It is common to hear that placing consumers on the board is an enlightened and correct thing to do. We disagree. Consumers can make very good board members, but only if they set aside their consumer hat in favor of their owner-representative hat. The portfolio of the consumer (or member of any other constituency) on the board should be defined to be just as broad as that of any other board member, that is, to stand in for the owners.

ASSIGNMENT: Discuss and decide whether the parts of this Levels Three, Four, and Five policy can stand alone (being sure to think of any policy as including all levels thus far) or needs further definition. If you desire more definition than provided in the levels shown, consider language even more detailed as you go on your own into further levels.

Board Committee Principles

Policy GP #2e states: *Board committees, when used, will be assigned so as to reinforce the wholeness of the board's job and so as never to interfere with delegation from board to CEO.* Tradition has encouraged boards to set up committees to advise, help, supervise, or be involved in virtually all areas of staff work. Boards that understand that the same job should not be delegated twice, or that inserting components of the board into staff functions renders the CEO less accountable, nonetheless may balk at the absoluteness of the rule expressed in the policy. Accordingly, many of our clients further define this policy to emphasize their determination to break with an insidious tradition before they delegate interpretation to their chair.

Policy GP #3e   Board Committee Principles: Level Three

1. Board committees are to help the board do its job, never to help or advise the staff. Committees ordinarily will assist the board by preparing policy alternatives and implications for board deliberation. In keeping with the board's broader focus, board committees will normally not have dealings with current staff operations.

2. Board committees may not speak or act for the board except when formally given such authority for specific and time-limited purposes. Expectations and authority will be carefully stated in order not to conflict with authority delegated to the CEO.

3. Board committees cannot exercise authority over staff. Because the CEO works for the full board, he or she will not be required to obtain approval of a board committee before an executive action.

4. Board committees are to avoid over-identification with organizational parts rather than the whole. Therefore a board committee that has helped the board create policy on some topic will not be used to monitor organizational performance on that same topic.

5. Committees will be used sparingly and ordinarily in an ad hoc capacity.

6. This policy applies to any group that is formed by board action, whether or not it is called a committee and regardless of whether the group includes board members. It does not apply to committees formed under the authority of the CEO.

Policy GP #3e leaves no doubt that board committees are instruments of governance, not of management. It also recognizes that the organization might have any number of committees that have nothing to do with the board. Parenthetically, we might add here that staff-formed committees can be made up partially or wholly of volunteers with no necessity whatsoever that these "worker" volunteers have a direct connection to the "governor" volunteers on the board.

Note that a board committee is defined as any committee formed by action by direct board authority, regardless of who is on the committee. In other words, the fact that the board "owns" a committee is what defines a board committee, not whether there are board members or others on the committee. Although not the topic at this point, the same rule is true for staff committees. That is, if a committee is formed by direct staff authority, it is a staff committee no matter who is on it.

In addition to a policy like this one on the principles by which a board will use committees, many boards find it useful as well to create a "Committee Structure" policy. Such a policy would describe each board committee quite explicitly in terms of (1) the *product* the committee is to produce and (2) the *authority* (in terms of use of organizational resources) it is granted. These two elements are vitally necessary to keep board committees effective. Hence, the policy might set up a committee to assist with the job of forming a linkage with the ownership; it might be charged crisply with the product of "alternative methods of establishing an inclusive community consultation" and the authority to use "fifty staff person hours and spend no more than $2,000."

ASSIGNMENT: Discuss and decide whether the parts of this Level Three policy can stand alone (being sure to think of any policy as including all levels thus far) or needs further definition. If you desire more definition than provided in Level Three, consider language even more detailed as you go on your own into Level Four policies or beyond.

Cost of Governance

Policy GP #2f states: *Because poor governance costs more than learning to govern well, the board will invest in its governance capacity.* This Level Two policy recognizes that governance unavoidably has a cost but that the costs of governing poorly are greater than the cost incurred in learning to govern well. Reference to investing in capability (increasing a certain kind of cost) is a commitment not to be penny-wise and pound-foolish. We suggest that straightforwardly dealing with board costs opens this matter up for discussion. One way to do this is to define the major cost areas and to allocate resources to those areas. We show further definition of this policy at Levels Three and Four.

Policy GP #3f Cost of Governance: Levels Three and Four

1. Board skills, methods, and supports will be sufficient to assure governing with excellence.

    a. Training and retraining will be used liberally to orient new members and candidates for membership, as well as to maintain and increase existing member skills and understandings.

    b. Outside monitoring assistance will be arranged so that the board can exercise confident control over organizational performance. This includes but is not limited to fiscal audit.

    c. Outreach mechanisms will be used as needed to ensure the board's ability to listen to owner viewpoints and values.

2. Costs will be prudently incurred, though not at the expense of endangering the development and maintenance of superior capability.

    a. Up to $_____ in fiscal year _____ for training, including attendance at conferences and workshops.

    b. Up to $_____ in fiscal year _____ for audit and other third-party monitoring of organizational performance.

    c. Up to $_____ in fiscal year _____ for surveys, focus groups, opinion analyses, and meeting costs.

Notice that these levels of detail spell out types and amounts of costs that the board expects to incur. The board that has been explicit about its own resource needs can instruct its CEO in Executive Limitations policy to ensure that the amount the board has specified will be available in the budget.

ASSIGNMENT: Discuss and decide whether the parts of this Level Three and Four policy can stand alone (being sure to think of any policy as including all levels thus far) or needs further definition. If you desire more definition than provided in the levels shown, consider language even more detailed as you go on your own into further levels.

Additional Governance Process Policies

Some boards work in special situations that require adding specialized policies to the more generic types listed in this chapter. We use one as an example.

Most hospital boards use their formal medical staff organization to assist them in assuring the quality of medical practice and of medical practitioners in the organization. From a strictly governance perspective, the organized medical staff is an important means with which the board would not normally involve itself. However, since the board is accountable for that which it cannot judge, that is, medical excellence, it requires assistance from those who are qualified to make such judgments. This phenomenon is not unlike the situation the board finds itself in with respect to financial issues. In that case, the board relies on qualified fiscal auditing firms. So a medical staff's enabling a board to be accountable is the medical equivalent of engaging an auditor. Theoretically, the board could obtain such assistance from any qualified source, but traditional practice is to use the hospital's own medical practitioner structure.

Such a decision requires that the board describe in a Governance Process policy how it will use the organized medical staff structure. A sample policy is shown next in two levels. Note that the board in question makes a clear distinction between the formal organization called *medical staff* and the individual practitioners who are members of that formal entity. Because we have not introduced this topic before, the sample policy that follows starts at Level Two, just below the general, largest-mixing-bowl policy.

Policy GP #2g: Charge to the Medical Staff: Levels Two and Three

The board's accountability for the quality of medical practice will be discharged in part by depending on the medical judgment of an organized Medical Staff. While the formal Medical Staff organization, consisting of all physicians privileged to practice in the organization, shall be responsible directly to the board, this does not relieve or otherwise affect the responsibility of individual physicians to requirements duly imposed by the CEO.

1. The Medical Staff will provide to the board its judgment as to the capability of relevant practices, personnel, and premises to support or provide quality care.

Figure 5.4. Governance Process Policies Completed.

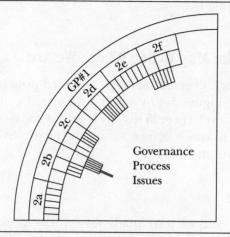

Note: Your Governance Process policies cover all possibilities (because they begin at the broadest level), yet extend to the board-desired level of specificity. Even with the chairperson having authority to use any reasonable interpretation of the policy words, the board can be said to be in control of its own products and process.

2. The Medical Staff will provide to the board its judgment as to the qualification of medical practitioners to render services and standards incumbent upon the organization or upon the Medical Staff.

3. The Medical Staff will provide the board with a representative summary of physician opinion by September 1 each year with respect to Ends deliberations of the board.

4. The Medical Staff will be held accountable by the board for its compliance with all laws, regulations, and standards that may be binding on the formal Medical Staff organization itself.

5. The Medical Staff will be accountable for an assessment of medical performance on the criteria above

    a. Annually by an internal examination by a mechanism established by the Medical Staff

    b. Not less than every three years by an external, disinterested third party of the board's choice, with whom the Medical Staff must fully cooperate

    c.   At any time the board deems it necessary by either internal or external audit.

Let's Check the Map to See Where We Are

The Governance Process category of board policies can now be represented in Figure 5.4 by a policy quadrant controlled all the way to at least Level Three. This has been the most common depth for our clients to reach before letting the chairperson handle further fleshing out in action.

Next Chapter

In our work so far, we have made assumptions about the board-CEO relationship. Now, in Chapter Six, we complete the policy category that describes that relationship: Board-CEO Linkage.

Chapter Six

Board-CEO Linkage Policies
Delegation to the CEO

In this chapter, we guide you through the policies used by the board to describe how it transfers a large portion of its authority to management. We call this category of board policies *Board-CEO Linkage,* but any similar title, such as "Board-Staff Connection" or "Governance-Management Relationship" would work as well. These policies deal with the methods and practices (means) of the board that describe not only the nature of delegation but the way in which the proper use of delegated authority is ascertained (monitoring).

This section of policy appears in the lower left-hand quadrant of the circle diagram as shown in Figure 6.1. Note that this quadrant does not describe *what* is delegated to the CEO but rather *how* delegation occurs. Hence this quadrant of policies does not instruct the CEO but is targeted at why the board has a CEO and how the board will behave in relating to the CEO.

Let's Take It from the Top: Level One

These policies start, as do all categories of board policy, with the most general, inclusive, and broad statement of the board's values. Our clients often form their first and broadest Board-CEO Linkage policy by defining the CEO position as the sole pathway between governance and operations. Your board can begin by examining the following example.

113

Figure 6.1. The Board-CEO Linkage Quadrant.

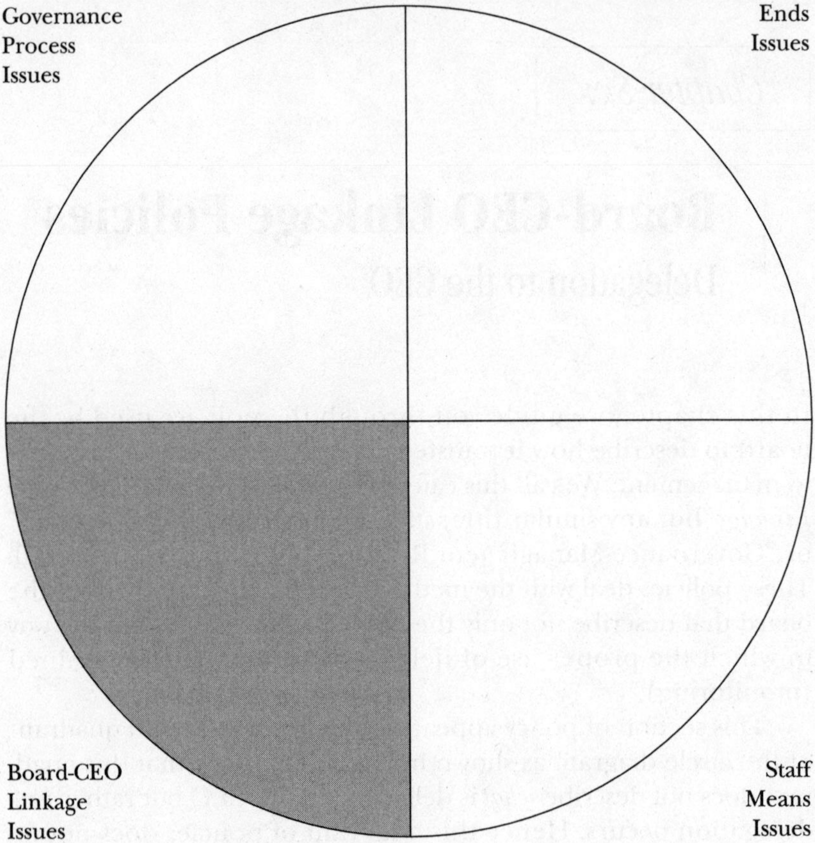

Governance
Process
Issues

Ends
Issues

Board-CEO
Linkage
Issues

Staff
Means
Issues

Note: On the circle diagram introduced in Chapter Two, policies dealt with in this chapter are in the lower left-hand quadrant.

Policy BCL #1: Global Board-CEO Linkage Policy

The board's sole official connection to the operating organization, its achievement, and conduct will be through a Chief Executive Officer.

We refer to this policy as BCL #1 for, as shown on the circle diagram in Figure 6.2, it is the most inclusive statement within this category. Although it is extremely general, note that it puts off-limits any other "paths" between board and operations for pur-

Figure 6.2. Board-CEO Linkage, Level One.

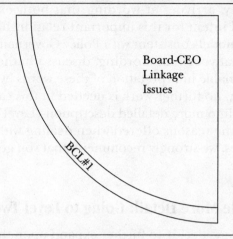

Board-CEO
Linkage
Issues

BCL #1

Note: At this point in our exercise, the outer level of the policy circle has been completed in the Board-CEO Linkage portion. The foundation for the governance-management relationship is established.

poses of organizational achievement and conduct. As is true for all the top-level policy statements, BCL #1 sets the stage for all further considerations in this category of board policies. For example, this simple statement would keep committees from being the path between board and staff. It also keeps the chairperson from being the path. The implication is that board committees and officers shall not get between the board and CEO. (To make no mistake about that interpretation, a Level Two statement will be offered later.) Figure 6.2 illustrates the capstone role played by BCL #1 in this category.

If your board is not intending to use a CEO position, it must devise some other way to assure accountability for organizational performance. It could hold separate persons accountable for separate domains of performance. It could hold committees accountable as groups for separate domains of performance. Both these alternatives, while difficult to avoid when there is no staff, cause the board a great deal of work. By far the most convenient choice for a board, even when the organization is small or the staff unpaid, is a CEO.

ASSIGNMENT: Discuss the wording of this Level One Board-CEO Linkage policy, arriving at wording that both expresses your board's global intent for this important relationship and, at the same time, is model-consistent with Policy Governance principles. After arriving at your final wording, discuss whether you can accept any reasonable interpretation of these words by the chairperson. If you can, no further work is needed in this category. If you cannot, going into more detailed description (Level Two) is called for. For the same reasons offered when dealing with Governance Process policies, we strongly recommend that you go at least as far as Level Three.

Here's a Little More Detail: Going to Level Two

Our clients always decide to further expand upon the meaning of this largest Board-CEO Linkage policy. In going into more detail, they define Level Two policies about a number of topics, usually the following:

- Unity of control—the CEO works only for the board as a body.
- Accountability of the CEO—CEO as embodiment of the organization.
- Delegation to the CEO—the nature of authorizing and instructing.
- Monitoring CEO performance—rules and process of evaluation.

Broad board statements about this second level of definition will be referred to as BCL #2 policies, and each will be assigned a letter, as in previous chapters. Let us review some examples of such Level Two policies.

ASSIGNMENT: Go through each of the following BCL #2 statements in turn, taking your time to discuss their implications for your board. Resist going into more detail at this time. Also, resist the temptation to word-craft commas and semicolons and grammar. Instead, examine your differences of opinion about the values expressed. Don't forget that each consideration that follows will have been preceded by the more general BCL #1 statement.

Policy BCL #2a: Unity of Control

Only decisions of the board acting as a body are binding on the CEO.

This policy baldly states the only condition under which the board's authority can be expressed, indeed, under which the board has any authority at all. Being unambiguous about this matter protects the board from the possible undermining of board authority by individual board members. It also protects the integrity of governance, in that the CEO and staff are less likely to respond to stray comments by individual board members, even when these board members are not trying to undermine board authority. Notice that it also protects the CEO from the renegade board member who would construe the CEO to be answerable to him or her.

ASSIGNMENT: Discuss and decide whether this policy is sufficient with respect to its topic or needs further definition. If this policy is sufficient, the chair will have the right to use any reasonable interpretation of its words. If you think further definition is needed, consider language described later in this chapter as Level Three policies.

Policy BCL #2b: Accountability of the CEO

The CEO is the board's only link to operational achievement and conduct, so that all authority and accountability of staff, as far as the board is concerned, is considered the authority and accountability of the CEO.

Policy BCL #2b clarifies that, from the board's perspective, the CEO and the organization are indivisible in terms of performance. Since the CEO is accountable for the success of the total organization, the matter of who does what on the staff is immaterial to the board. Using this approach, it is not possible to have a successful organization and a poor CEO, or an unsuccessful organization and a good CEO. Does your board understand that in order for this policy to be truly followed, the board must never instruct persons who report to the CEO? Does it consider that the wording of this policy at Level Two adequately describes the powerful yet controlled nature of its delegation? It may wish to further define its terms before allowing the chair to interpret its words. If so, a Level Three policy is required.

ASSIGNMENT: Discuss and decide whether this policy is sufficient with respect to its topic or needs further definition. If this policy is sufficient, the chair will have the right to use any reasonable interpretation of its words. If you think further definition is needed, consider language described later in this chapter as Level Three policies.

Policy BCL #2c: Delegation to the CEO

The board will instruct the CEO through written policies that prescribe the organizational Ends to be achieved and describe organizational situations and actions to be avoided, allowing the CEO to use any reasonable interpretation of these policies.

You will have noticed that this policy demands rigorous board discipline. It commits the board to a number of practices that, if followed, totally change board behavior. First, the requirement to write down instructions is vital if a group is going to act as a body. After all, it is impossible to know what a group has said unless it writes its words and agrees to them. Second, using discipline to stay positive about ends and negative about means demands a rigor that both clarifies expectations and allows for meaningful CEO understanding of the job to be done. This policy also clearly acknowledges that words must be interpreted and assigns the right to interpret them to the CEO. Is your board ready to undertake such a powerful and unambiguous delegation? Policy Governance enables your board to delegate in this manner *safely*.

ASSIGNMENT: Discuss and decide whether this is sufficient with respect to its topic or needs further definition. If this policy is sufficient, the chair will have the right to use any reasonable interpretation of its words. If you think further definition is needed, consider language described later in this chapter as Level Three policies.

Policy BCL #2d: Monitoring CEO Performance

Systematic and rigorous monitoring of CEO job performance will be solely against the only expected CEO job outputs: organizational accomplishment of board policies on Ends and organizational operation within the boundaries established in board policies on Executive Limitations.

Boards have traditionally found CEO evaluation to be a difficult task. We are sure that the difficulty they have experienced
stems from their failure to produce criteria against which monitoring can take place. Put another way, deciding *what is expected*
must precede monitoring. This policy clarifies that the requirements stated by the board in Ends and Executive Limitations policies *are the criteria* for CEO evaluation. We discuss monitoring in
depth later in this chapter. The purpose of this chapter section is
to demonstrate how the board expresses its intention to handle the
monitoring of the CEO.

The board's obligation to evaluate organizational performance
can only be met by evaluating its CEO against criteria the board
has previously set. The implication of such a requirement is that
there can be no evaluation of a CEO job and, in fact, there can be
no defined CEO job outputs at all, until the board has completed
its obligation to clearly articulate its requirements. Is your board
prepared to exercise the discipline required to strictly adhere to
such a policy? How could it justify anything else? As to the depth
of this policy making about monitoring, our experience is that
boards wish to go into much more detail in describing their monitoring methods and in devising an actual schedule of monitoring
before handing off to the chair.

ASSIGNMENT: Discuss and decide whether this policy is sufficient
with respect to its topic or needs further definition. If this policy is
sufficient, the chair will have the right to use any reasonable interpretation of its words. If you think further definition is needed,
consider language described later in this chapter as Level Three
policies.

Let's Check the Map to See Where We Are

Now you have completed Level Two policies in the Board-CEO
Linkage category of board policies. While we recommend that your
board define still further, what has now been produced constitutes
a complete overview of the CEO's job, his or her relation to the
board's work, and the wholeness of the board in that relationship.
Once again, let's return to the policy circle in Figure 6.3 to visual-
ize this new layer of policy.

Figure 6.3. Board-CEO Linkage, Levels One and Two.

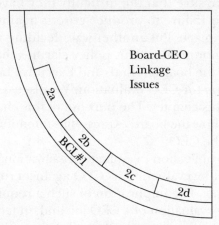

Note: With policy language at the BCL #2 level, the initial, global description of this relationship has now been further defined with respect to a few critical dimensions.

ASSIGNMENT: Look over your work so far. You have now created one BCL #1 global policy and several further refinements at the BCL #2 level. As further interpreted by the chairperson, these policies put both board and CEO on notice about the nature of this important relationship. You will have further opportunity to make the policies more specific (Level Three), but these Level Two policies provide the foundation upon which any further specifics are based.

Going into Even More Detail: Level Three

In the following pages, we demonstrate some Level Three policies (BCL #3). As before, Level Three further defines the words of Level Two. Remember that Level Two policies were themselves built upon the Level One policy that started this sequence.

Unity of Control

Policy BCL #2a states: *Only decisions of the board acting as a body are binding on the CEO.* This policy states broadly the principle that only the board as a body may instruct the CEO and that the CEO is accountable for meeting only the expectations expressed by the whole board. This point seems unambiguous enough, but examine the following embellishments to see the additional definition they contribute.

Policy BCL #3a   Unity of Control: Level Three

1. Decisions or instructions of individual board members, officers, or committees are not binding on the CEO except in rare instances when the board has specifically authorized such exercise of authority.

2. In the case of board members or committees requesting information or assistance without board authorization, the CEO can refuse such requests that require, in the CEO's opinion, a material amount of staff time or funds, or are disruptive.

This policy makes clear that board members have no power to act as individuals in the organization. Its second section introduces a new implication for many boards. Often board members fail to realize that individually demanding information from staff is, in fact, a unilateral commandeering of resources. Most boards have no idea what one or more of their colleagues cost the organization in staff time to research questions. The reason the board chooses in this policy to "save" the CEO from individual requests is not to make life easier for the CEO but to protect its own group authority. Individual board members can surely get their questions answered unless their doing so burdens the organization. The board as a body, of course, can get any question answered it chooses.

ASSIGNMENT: Discuss and decide whether the parts of this Level Three policy can stand alone (being sure to think of any policy as including all levels thus far) or need further definition. If you desire more definition than provided in Level Three, consider language even more detailed as you go on your own into Level Four policies or beyond.

Accountability of the CEO

Policy BCL #2b states: *The CEO is the board's only official link to operational achievement and conduct, so that all authority and accountability of staff, as far as the board is concerned, is considered the authority and accountability of the CEO.* This policy clearly establishes the pivotal role of the CEO. We have found that the details of a Level Three policy are useful to boards, and we recommend that you consider the following policy sample:

Policy BCL #3b   Accountability of the CEO: Level Three

1. The board will never give instructions to persons who report directly or indirectly to the CEO.

2. The board will refrain from evaluating, either formally or informally, any staff other than the CEO.

3. The board will view CEO performance as identical to organizational performance so that organizational accomplishment of board-stated Ends and avoidance of board-proscribed means will be viewed as successful CEO performance.

These provisions are straightforward, to be sure, but your board will profit from a discussion of its proper relationship to non-CEO staff. Note that this policy does not prohibit contact and interaction but does require the board to avoid even informally instructing or evaluating these staff. Can you see the usefulness to all board members of clarifying these issues?

ASSIGNMENT: Discuss and decide whether the parts of this Level Three policy can stand alone (being sure to think of any policy as including all levels thus far) or need further definition. If you desire more definition than provided in Level Three, consider language even more detailed as you go on your own into Level Four policies or beyond.

Delegation to the CEO

Policy BCL #2c states: *The board will instruct the CEO through written policies that prescribe the organizational Ends to be achieved and describe organizational situations and actions to be avoided, allowing the CEO to use any reasonable interpretation of these policies.* Our clients commonly decide to define this policy further, since it differs so markedly from standard board practice. They wish to be explicit in describing the "go 'til we say stop" manner of their delegation, since they are aware that the traditional manner of delegating is "stop 'til we say go." Taken together with the Level Two portion of this topic, the combined BCL #2c-3c policy is a succinct treatise on CEO delegation in the Policy Governance model.

Policy BCL #3c   Delegation to the CEO: Level Three

1. The board will develop policies instructing the CEO to achieve certain results, for certain recipients at a specified cost. These policies will be developed systematically from the broadest, most general level to more defined levels and will be called *Ends policies*.

2. The board will develop policies that limit the latitude the CEO may exercise in choosing the organizational means. These policies will be developed systematically from the broadest, most general level to more defined levels, and they will be called *Executive Limitations policies*.

3. As long as the CEO uses any reasonable interpretation of the board's Ends and Executive Limitations policies, the CEO is authorized to establish all further policies, make all decisions, take all actions, establish all practices, and develop all activities.

4. The board may change its Ends and Executive Limitations policies, thereby shifting the boundary between board and CEO domains. By doing so, the board changes the latitude of choice given to the CEO. But as long as any particular delegation is in place, the board will respect and support the CEO's choices.

These provisions more finely describe the method the board will use to empower the CEO position. They describe the way that CEO authority is packaged.

ASSIGNMENT: Discuss and decide whether the parts of this Level Three policy can stand alone (being sure to think of any policy as including all levels thus far) or need further definition. If you desire more definition than provided in Level Three, consider language even more detailed as you go on your own into Level Four policies or beyond.

Monitoring CEO Performance

Policy BCL #2d states: *Systematic and rigorous monitoring of CEO job performance will be solely against the only expected CEO job outputs: organizational accomplishment of board policies on Ends and organizational operation within the boundaries of board policies on Executive Limitations.* This policy, which emphasizes that CEO performance is exactly the same as organizational performance, introduces the strict definition of monitoring used in Policy Governance. The board is required to state its criteria for organizational success, to whatever detail it chooses, using the ends-means distinction. It is then obliged to monitor that reasonable interpretations of its requirements were met. The board's written policies are the *only* criteria that may be used.

Having established this important principle, many boards wish to enumerate the methods by which they may obtain the monitoring data they need, thereby not leaving the mechanics to chair choice. Some also wish to enlarge upon their definition of monitoring itself. Accordingly, it is common to see Level Three and Four policies about monitoring.

Policy BCL #3d   Monitoring CEO Performance: Levels Three and Four

1. Monitoring is simply to determine the degree to which board policies are being met. Data that do not do this will not be considered to be monitoring data.

2. The board will acquire monitoring data by one or more of three methods: (a) by internal report, in which the CEO discloses compliance information to the board, (b) by external report, in which an external, disinterested third party selected by the board assesses compliance with board policies, and (c) by direct board inspection, in which a designated member or members of the board assess compliance with the appropriate policy criteria.

3. In every case, the standard for compliance shall be *any reasonable CEO interpretation* of the board policy being monitored.

4. All policies that instruct the CEO will be monitored at a frequency and by a method chosen by the board. The board can monitor any policy at any time by any method, but will ordinarily depend on a routine schedule.

Policy	Method	Frequency
Treatment of Consumers	Internal	Annually
Treatment of Staff	Internal	Annually
Financial Planning and Budgeting	Internal	Quarterly
Financial Condition and Activities	Internal	Quarterly
	External	Annually
Emergency CEO Succession	Internal	Annually
Compensation and Benefits	Internal	Annually
	External	Biannually
Communication and Support	Direct Inspection	Annually

You will remember that the Executive Limitations policy Communication and Support to the Board requires that the CEO provide to the board the monitoring information spelled out in its monitoring schedule. Section 4 of this policy is where that monitoring schedule can be found. Of course, the only portions incumbent upon the CEO to provide are those marked "internal report." This policy, therefore, defines what monitoring is, explains alternate methods that the board can use to carry it out, and further specifically establishes the board's expectations for the receipt of monitoring information.

The monitoring schedule shown includes only policies of the Executive Limitations category, since at this time no Ends policies have been developed. It is important, of course, that as Ends policies are created, they are placed into this schedule to ensure proper monitoring. We have chosen methods and frequencies that correspond roughly to those our clients often use. Your board, however, should discuss which methods (that is, those methods listed in Section 2 of this policy) and frequencies would satisfy its continual need for assurance, bearing in mind the cost of monitoring. As you see in the case of Financial Condition and Activities, the board can select more than one method for a given policy. The "external" report in this case would be that typically done by an outside auditing firm.

ASSIGNMENT: Discuss and decide whether this policy can stand alone (being sure to think of any policy as including all levels thus far) or needs further definition. If you desire more definition than shown here, consider language even more detailed as you go on your own into further levels.

Let's Check the Map to See Where We Are

The Board-CEO Linkage policies now describe the governance-management connection in a more powerful, clear way. Now that we have completed a round of Level Three policies, let's see in Figure 6.4 how that policy circle is looking.

ASSIGNMENT: Look over your work so far. You have now created a rather complete set of Board-CEO Linkage policies. Do these make sense as a whole in describing an empowering and fair, yet rigorous, relationship between the functions of governance and management? Have you been careful to stick carefully to Policy Governance principles as you tailored the policy samples?

Figure 6.4. Board-CEO Linkage Policies Completed.

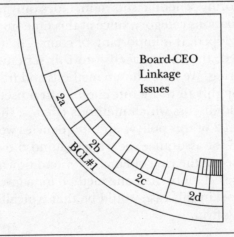

Note: With a more or less full complement of Board-CEO Linkage policies in place, your board policies lack only the important Ends category to be complete.

Take a Closer Look at Monitoring

This chapter, like those that precede it, is written chiefly to guide you through the details of policy making. Policy making in the Board-CEO Linkage category includes creating board policy about the monitoring or evaluation process. Basically, this aspect deals with how the board can assure itself whether everything is in order, that is, whether the operational organization is performing satisfactorily.

The history of boards and monitoring has been so steeped in poor governance practice, however, that we regularly find boards having trouble with this part of their obligation, even with the simplification that Policy Governance affords. For that reason we add this section to help your board think soundly about monitoring. These thoughts about the practicalities of monitoring will make it easier to stick with the policy you've already written. We begin by restating the role played by monitoring in the larger scheme of accountability.

Accountability requires (1) setting expectations, (2) assigning performance to someone, and (3) checking to see if the expectations are met. By and large, when boards have trouble with monitoring, the difficulty exists in having not completed the first step first (setting expectations). In Policy Governance, *everything* the board expects of the CEO and, therefore, everything the board has any reasonable prerogative to monitor is stated in Ends and Executive Limitations policies. The board's monitoring stance with respect to the CEO, then, is simply to inspect whether the CEO has given the board what it wants (Ends) and has avoided what the board doesn't want (Executive Limitations). Proper monitoring must be this and *only* this.

The question of Ends monitoring frequently worries our clients. They surmise correctly that exact measurement of Ends is difficult and, in some cases, impossible. They wonder how they can be sure that the organization has accomplished the prescribed Ends. "How do we know if we made a difference?" they ask us. Our first response is often, "How do you know now?" Your board probably realizes at this point in the book that it simply does not know what your organizational impact is now. It is important to be aware of how little you know now, because we are going to confirm your suspicion that you will not achieve pristine measures of Ends accomplishment. You will write Ends policies in the detail you require before allowing your CEO to use any reasonable interpretation of your words. The CEO must then assure you with data that a reasonable interpretation was achieved. This will be a crude measure. But it will be a crude measure of the right thing!

We have found that in the area of monitoring, boards often drift off-course rapidly when they begin to implement Policy Governance. We therefore review here some of the usual mistakes we have encountered when boards struggle with the very necessary job of monitoring CEO performance. We then describe a technique we have found helpful in rapidly establishing a monitoring schedule.

1. *The policies are the criteria.* It is perhaps because boards are traditionally so remiss in clarifying their expectations that new Policy Governance boards find it hard to remember that in making Ends and Executive Limitations policies, they have just established all the criteria they need. We have seen boards conscientiously struggle with and decide upon these policies, and then set up additional "monitoring requirements," some of which bear no relationship to the policies. They proceed to receive reports on a number of items and review them in the absence of any standards of acceptability known to them or, of course, to the CEO.

One such example was the board that required reports on employment equity, staff orientation, and a number of other staff-related matters. When asked how they would judge these reports after having received them, the board had to acknowledge that it had no board-stated expectations at all in these areas, except that the law be observed. Meanwhile, the laboriously developed staff treatment policy (which, of course, did state expectations) was going unmonitored!

In another example, a board of a college carefully defined the required student achievement and then received so-called monitoring reports tracking the number of students enrolled in a certain selection of classes. Social service organizations occasionally make this error also, mistaking the numbers of people attending their programs and services (which are means) for monitoring data about Ends.

In both examples, the board was receiving information that may have been interesting but was not monitoring any criteria in existence. There is nothing wrong with the board knowing about these data, but to think of them as monitoring cheats the integrity of governance.

2. *The monitoring of criteria is a passive process that is different from the setting of criteria.* We have encountered boards that, having failed to monitor the criteria they have set, find themselves examining information about which they have no criteria, and establishing criteria "on the fly." Monitoring in Policy Governance is simply the comparison of what is to what was (or what was not) required. (Notice that traditional budget approval or financial report approval are instances of on-the-fly criteria setting.) The only judgment applied to true monitoring data is simply to determine whether the data demonstrate a reasonable interpretation of the requirement set out in policy.

3. *"Any reasonable interpretation" means just that.* New Policy Governance boards occasionally forget that they have allowed the CEO to use any reasonable interpretation of their words. Board members find themselves judging the monitoring data they receive against the standard of their own personal preference. "Would I have made that decision?" is a different question from, "Is that decision or outcome a reasonable interpretation of what we said?" The first compares CEO performance to an unstated and individually determined criterion, exactly the shoot-from-the-hip comparison that the board has determined not to make! The latter compares CEO performance to a group expectation that was previously known.

A variant of this mistake in monitoring occurs when board members defer to the opinion of the board expert (either real or self-proclaimed) on the subject at hand. Needing to please the expert on the board is a different requirement than needing to prove one has performed a reasonable interpretation of board policy.

Another version of this monitoring mistake occurs when the board finds that the CEO made a decision that *none of the board members like* and, because of this, decide that the CEO is out of compliance. While this board opinion is an interesting phenomenon, it does not establish CEO wrong-doing, since the crucial judgment is the one still pending: Is the decision a reasonable interpretation of board policy? Of course, it is possible for a CEO decision to be a reasonable interpretation of board policy and still be a decision the board does not like. But this situation says nothing about CEO performance (except to congratulate it). It indicates that the board needs either to change or to further define its policy, leaving a new range of interpretation that the board can live with. In other words, in such an instance, the error is in board policy, not in the CEO.

4. *Policy violation can mean one of several things.* When a board has found that a policy has not been accorded a reasonable interpretation by the CEO, it must examine a number of possibilities. It may be that the policy, while appropriate and doable when set, is no longer a realistic requirement. If this is the case, the board will want to change its policy. It may be that the violation is the result of a temporary and insignificant "blip" and will be righted immediately. The board may decide to take no action about such a violation, other than noting it. Or it may be that the CEO is performing below the level required by the board.

5. *The board is not there to help the CEO but to instruct and monitor the CEO.* When a board finds that its CEO is performing below the required standards, it is sometimes tempted to fix, or to help the CEO fix, the problem. This is precisely the wrong thing to do, as it makes the board unable to hold the CEO accountable for fixing a problem and keeping it fixed. Accordingly, in the case of a policy infraction, the board must decide if it can wait the amount of time the CEO feels will be needed to restore functioning to criterion level. If it can, it should monitor that the problem has indeed been fixed within the time allowed. If it cannot, it should consider replacing the CEO.

This is occasionally difficult for board members to understand, especially if some of them are managers in their own right. Managers know that management includes coaching and helping staff. Governors must learn that governance differs from management; the accountability placed on the CEO is not a burden that can be lifted from the CEO without serious damage to the board's overall accountability for the organization. Naturally, the CEO who is held accountable for policy compliance can request from individuals the help he or she needs in order to deliver to the board what is required. The CEO can even request help from individual board members if he or she feels they are the most appropriate helpers. But allowing the decision about the need for help and the choice of helper to be freely made by the CEO enables the board to continue to hold the CEO accountable.

6. *The question must be answered.* Unbelievably, we have encountered boards that fail to truly examine their monitoring reports to determine if they show that a reasonable interpretation of the policies was achieved. They accept reports that do not answer the questions posed by the policies. There are two variants of this problem. One is when the board accepts reports that are full of data but that do not address policy criteria at all. We have seen boards accept pages and pages of financial data purporting to monitor the requirement that the organization not spend more money than it had received in the fiscal year to date. But boards only require two numbers to monitor this policy provision, and mountains of information can serve to obscure the answer to this relatively easy, but important, means question. Remember that too much information is much worse than none; having none is hard to miss, while having too much may be falsely reassuring.

The second variant occurs when the board accepts a report that affirms compliance without providing data. We have seen reports submitted by CEOs that merely include a statement by the CEO that everything is in order. These reports are of the "trust me" variety, disclosing nothing of substance to the board. Only more amazing than the CEO who submits such a report is the board that accepts it. We are not advising against the CEO personally "certifying" or assuring that policy provisions have been met, just that such an assurance cannot not pass muster in the absence of presenting data as well.

7. *If a policy is worth stating, it is worth monitoring.* We have occasionally been surprised by a board balking at the need to institute rigorous monitoring of its criteria. Often the objection raised centers around the perception that a great deal of staff time will be used in preparing reports for the board. Traditional boards expressing such concerns forget that their staff already prepare huge amounts of information for them, information that does not relate at all to any stated expectations the board may have and that could be described as hundreds of answers looking around desperately for ten good questions.

There is no doubt that some staff time must be spent in preparing for the board reports that demonstrate organizational performance as measured against board criteria. Boards certainly should be careful not to demand reports from staff that they don't actually need. But a Policy Governance board that has made its policies carefully, defining its requirements to the level at which it can accept any reasonable interpretation by the CEO, has a set of rules that it has itself determined to be necessary. If it is necessary to set such rules, it is necessary to check them too! Remember that the board must state the frequency with which its criteria are to be monitored. There is no need for it to demand reports at a high frequency if it will be satisfied by a lower frequency. This also will limit the time staff spend in report writing.

Setting the Monitoring Schedule

Sometimes the monitoring problem for a board is simply not going ahead and doing it! We recommend establishing a schedule for monitoring as soon as possible after crafting the Executive Limitations policies. Go about doing that in three steps, each of which we outline. Then place the monitoring schedule you will have developed into the Monitoring CEO Performance policy (shown earlier in this chapter) as subparts of Section Four. Here is the method we use. Try it.

1. Using a flip chart or other group recording method, list in a first column all the Executive Limitations policies. Show a column two headed "method" and a column three headed "frequency."

2. Now begin at the top of your list and answer the question for each policy, What source of monitoring data do we want?

    a. Let us suggest that with each policy, you begin with an assumption that internal report will be the method. It is the cheapest and, as it turns out, the most common monitoring source. With that as a point of departure, see if anyone can make a strong enough case for external report or direct inspection to get a majority of votes for either of those. We recommend you use direct inspection sparingly if at all.

b. Be aware that at this stage, you might want to have more than one method or source per policy, but at different frequencies. For example, it is common for Policy Governance boards to monitor their Financial Condition and Activities policy once a month or quarter with data from the CEO (internal report) and once annually from a board-appointed auditor (external report).

3. Taking one policy at a time again, consider only the frequency of monitoring. Just answer the question, How often must we see monitoring data about this policy in order to feel confident about CEO performance? Here is how you can quickly determine your monitoring frequencies:

a. Ask, "How many board members would be satisfied with once per year?" Perhaps a hand or two will go up. Ask those persons to leave their hands up as you go on to the next step.

b. Ask, "How many of you would be satisfied with twice per year?" A few more hands will go up, joining the first ones. All hands in the air should stay in the air as you go on to the next step.

c. Ask the same question for quarterly, then for monthly, at each point making sure that hands that are up from an earlier query have stayed up. When this cumulative voting method reaches a criterion level (usually a simple majority), you have ascertained the monitoring frequency for the policy in question!

As End policies are developed, use the same technique to define method and frequency of monitoring. Add these new determinations to your Monitoring CEO Performance policy. You may have noticed that our sample policy of that title shows a monitoring schedule that looks just like your flip chart version. For those policies monitored by internal reports, the provision of your Communication and Support to the Board policy ensures that the data will begin to flow to the board without your having even to think about the matter after this point. For those policies monitored by either external report or direct inspection, the board will have to devise some scheme by which that will occur. If the board fails to do this, the chair simply inherits the job, using any reasonable interpretation of whatever the board has said about the subject.

In summary, then, the Board-CEO Linkage policies establish three important components of the accountable organization:

1. A carefully crafted method whereby the board expresses its expectations for the operational organization.
2. A powerfully simple avenue along which authority and accountability flow from the full board to one individual (the CEO).
3. A thorough but fair evaluative stance vis-à-vis the CEO: *all* official instructions will be monitored, and *only* official instructions will be monitored in determining CEO job performance.

Next Chapter

At this point in your work, all policy categories have been completed except the most exciting and compelling one of all, Ends. In Chapter Seven, we help you begin this important process. While Executive Limitations, Governance Process, and Board-CEO Linkage categories can be completed relatively quickly, Ends require more study and creativity. They are the central challenge to board decision making.

Ends Policies
The Real Bottom Line

In this chapter, we are going to guide you through the process of developing the Ends policies of your organization. Although this challenge will be the heart of the board's work forever, it is not necessary to finish your Ends work prior to putting the other three categories of policies into effect.

Policies in the other three categories should be relatively complete in order to codify the board's job and the board's relationship with management, as well as to provide the safety to "let go" afforded by Executive Limitations. But with those policies in place, the board and CEO can begin operating in a Policy Governance manner. We refer you to Chapter Nine for tips on getting that process started.

The work of this chapter, however, is to describe the board's never-ending task of determining not what the organization does but what it is for. Our attention turns, then, to the creation of Ends. *Ends* in Policy Governance refers to the effect an organization seeks to have on the world outside itself. It will cause something to be different for someone at some cost. The concept *ends* embraces:

- The impact, difference, change, benefit, or outcome to be obtained in the lives of consumers or consumer-like populations. Let's call this *results*.
- The identity, description, or characteristics of the consumers or populations to receive the results. Let's call these *recipients*.
- The monetary expense, relative worth, or relative priority of a result or set of results, or the comparative priority of certain

recipients rather than others getting the results. Let's call this feature *cost*.

Ends policies, then, are policies that address a threefold concept: your organization's results, recipients, and cost of results. To qualify as an ends statement, a proposition must describe at least one of the three components. Taken as a whole, of course, your Ends policies will describe all three. We intentionally risk overkill in defining the ends concept, for we have found that despite its simplicity, it is persistently misinterpreted. *We strongly urge compulsive attention to the ends definition.*

You will sometimes hear ends mistakenly equated with results only. Be careful not to fall into this trap, as the concept is broader than a simple designation of outcome. (If results were the only meaning of ends, there would have been no need for using a word other than *results* in the first place.) You will find yourself tempted to define ends as anything that is important, required by law, or the end point of a process. None of these are correct definitions. You will find yourself tempted to define ends as your programs, services, or curricula. These are not ends; they are packages of means. Fiscal soundness and a good budget are means also. You will find yourself calling all of these *ends* occasionally. Watch out for this! We suggest that board members develop a habit of friendly but rigorous policing of each other in order that the concept not deteriorate with misuse.

Ends issues are located on the circle diagram in the top right-hand quadrant, as shown in Figure 7.1.

As with all other policy types, Ends are developed beginning from the broadest, most inclusive and general level first, then toward progressively more defined levels. Also in common with the other policy types, they are developed to the point that the board can accept any reasonable interpretation of a delegatee. In this case, the delegatee is the CEO.

Despite these features in common with the other policy types, this chapter will be very different from the three preceding chapters. For policy development within Executive Limitations, Governance Process, and Board-CEO Linkage (all means policies), we were able to present you with some generic samples. Those policies were model-consistent examples of what many boards have

Figure 7.1. The Ends Quadrant.

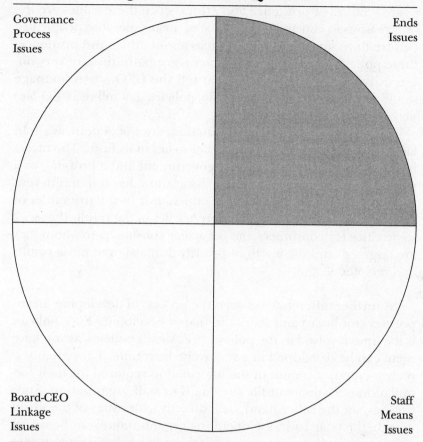

Governance
Process
Issues

Ends
Issues

Board-CEO
Linkage
Issues

Staff
Means
Issues

Note: On the circle diagram introduced in Chapter Two, the policies dealt with in this chapter are in the upper right-hand quadrant.

used. While we expect that you will have changed them somewhat, the format and content of means policies have general applicability across organizations of all types.

• Governance Process and Board-CEO Linkage policies describe both the Policy Governance model and its practical application. If you accept the model, your policies in these categories will merely be slightly tailored restatements of the model itself.

- Executive Limitations policies are really an expression of the board's values of prudence and ethics, since these values are the only reasons to constrain the choice of means. Because people in a culture have somewhat similar ideas about ethics and prudence, these policies tend to be similar across organizations of very different types. (While policies that tell the CEO *how* to manage would not be generically applicable, policies that tell the CEO *how not* to manage are.)
- Ends policies, in sharp distinction, are not generic at all. In fact, the uniqueness of any organization lies in its Ends. The meaningful difference between a city government and a hospital, or a mental health center and a trade association, lies not in different concepts of what is prudent and ethical nor in the principles of governance. The meaningful difference lies in the results they seek to produce for consumers, the particular consumers to whom they are targeted, and the worth or priority they assign to those results and recipients.

A further difference between the process of developing means policies (for board and staff) and that of developing Ends policies is the time involved in the policy work. Means policies, as you have seen, can be developed in a relatively short time. They are internally focused, and most of the information required for their formulation is available inside the board or staff organization. Ends policies, on the other hand, deal directly with issues of the world outside the board and the operating organization. Your board, in making its Ends policies, will be making hard choices about who will and who will not benefit from your organization, and in what ways. Such decisions are difficult, perhaps painful, and may be politically charged. They always need to be made with proper diligence from a very informed position, for a board makes such determinations on behalf not of itself, or its staff, or even today's consumers, but on behalf of the ownership in general.

Hence, we are not able to present you with samples of Ends policies that you can work from, as we did in the other policy quadrants. What this chapter will do is provide a format, or a sequence, for your board to use when it involves itself in the long and difficult task of Ends policy development.

When your board sets out on its Ends work, approach the task with the following perspectives:

1. *Don't assume that your existing mission statement is an Ends policy.* We often find that our clients have inspiring and rhetorically attractive mission statements, and we do not at all mean to minimize either the effort that went into preparing such documents or their possible public relations value. It is rare, however, that they are written in ends terminology, that is, that they define who is to benefit from the organization, in what way, or at what cost. They therefore do not qualify as Ends policies.

2. *Expect it to be difficult.* This may be counterintuitive. Our clients often start the policy development process expecting that means policies will be difficult to write and that Ends policies will be easy. After all, they reason, it's pretty obvious why the organization exists. After not very long, they realize it is not at all obvious what benefits should accrue, much less to which consumers at what cost. It is clear that boards have seldom considered such issues and that, as a result, they need to start virtually from scratch to define organizational purpose.

3. *Be rigorous about Ends attributes.* This is difficult at first, since you will find that it feels more natural to describe activities and intentions than to prescribe results, recipients, and cost. In time, you will get used to speaking in ends terminology, but for this to happen, you must learn to recognize that effort and action words almost always describe means, not ends. If you prescribe means to your staff, you will surely get them, but you will still be in the dark as to whether the right results were produced for the right people at the right cost.

4. *Never assume that your existing strategic plan is or contains Ends policy.* You may have spent some time developing a strategic plan. These plans usually contain a number of goals, objectives, or strategies for future years. Our experience is that they almost always are means documents. Plans, after all, describe how to get from here to there. Ends policies describe "there" with a consumer benefit focus. It only illustrates the aimless means focus of many nonprofit and governmental organizations that it is common to have extensive strategic planning even though ends are largely undefined! In

Policy Governance, the CEO has the same prerogatives with strategic planning as with any other staff means issue: he or she must make sure that all planning is within constraints placed on him or her by the board.

5. *Develop Ends policies with a long-term perspective.* Your board should aim at defining what the organization is to accomplish, for whom, and at what cost over the next several years, not by next month. Using a horizon that is appropriately distant will force the board to have a future orientation and to inform itself about future developments in the profile of needs and populations. It also recognizes that the staff needs time to plan and implement change in pursuit of the board's Ends.

6. *Make sure Ends are doable.* Ends policies, even at the most global level, describe the achievements for which the CEO will be held accountable. Accordingly, the board must be careful to make its requirements realistically ambitious. You should expect the maximum *possible,* not the maximum conceivable. So avoid rhetorical flourish. "A world that works for everyone," "A community free of alcoholism," or "*Every* child a wanted child" are Ends statements, but probably not yours! These are ideal states to which your board may have a philosophical commitment and, for that reason, bear stating. In other words, your board may want to make a statement of philosophy or be explicit about its motivation or the beliefs that bring it together in the first place. This is understandable, but such statements are not Ends. They belong in the Governance Process quadrant of board policy, declaring, in effect, where the board is "coming from" or the board's mentality.

7. *Ignore current organizational divisions or departments.* Your board should not make Ends policy on a department-by-department basis. Remember that the organizational structure, or division of labor, is a staff means issue and has been delegated to the CEO. The CEO has the right, unless specifically constrained by Executive Limitations policies, to change internal organizational structure. Do not allow staff structure to drive board thinking about the impact your organization should have.

8. *Never allow the problem of measurement to come up as you decide Ends.* We are aware of how odd this sounds. We, too, have heard the rules about always having measurable objectives. We are not opposed to measurement! We are simply asserting that if the board

allows measurement questions to contaminate its deliberations about what is to be accomplished, for whom, and at what cost, it will prescribe what is measurable rather than what is meaningful. We urge you to demand meaningful performance from your organization. The CEO will be required to convince the board that a reasonable interpretation of the board's Ends demands was delivered. So let measurement be the CEO's problem, but be realistically prepared to accept crude measures. It would be wonderful if Ends could be precisely measured, but at this stage of history they will likely be measured only crudely. A useful adage to remember states, "A crude measure of the right thing beats a precise measure of the wrong thing." For too long, our nonprofit and public organizations have been precisely measuring the wrong things!

9. *Expect to find that there is information you need and don't have.* Policy Governance boards spend a large amount of time getting educated. To demand doable results, to specify recipients, and to set acceptable costs raise many difficult questions. Just what is doable? Who are the potential consumers for whom we could make a difference, and how do we choose among them? What choices do our owners want us to make, and how will we deal with the inevitability that the owners themselves don't agree? How much should the results we demand cost? How should the results we seek change over the next few years? How will changes in public policy affect our choices? You can undoubtedly think of many more examples of information required for Ends decisions.

Now with those observations in mind, let us proceed through a set of exercises aimed at assisting your board to find the broadest, most inclusive, largest-mixing-bowl Ends policy for your organization. In order to do these exercises, it would help to appoint a member of the board to use a flip chart so that the various attempts that your board makes can be kept together. We strongly urge that all board members be involved in this exercise.

Let's Take It from the Top: Level One

Your board will start its Ends policy development by deciding on the largest appropriate Ends statement.

We have found that focusing on the results aspect of ends is a good start-up strategy. That is, don't try to cover results, recipients, and cost all in this beginning exercise. Not having to focus on recipients and cost makes the job easier at this juncture. You might find that specification of recipients will occasionally emerge naturally. If it does so, fine, but our initial focus will be results.

Let's give this approach a rational grounding as well as a practical one. Results precede the other two components. Organizations exist to cause something to be different. What is the difference? What is your organization for, stated in its simplest and most focused form? In other words, what should result from organizational activity? What does it produce? For this reason we'll look for getting a handle on results first.

Only then will we concern ourselves with who gets the results. Ostensibly, your organization can't produce its results for the whole world. Some populations or individuals will get the benefits, and some will not. Who should benefit? How will the benefits be apportioned?

Finally, we concern ourselves with what these results with these people are worth. What are they worth in monetary terms? What are they worth in opportunity cost, that is, other things given up in order to get them? Or what is their importance relative to each other rather than relative to money or opportunities foregone? In other words, what are their relative priorities?

This succession of questions (what results, next which people, finally what cost) can be asked at all levels of abstraction. That is, they can be asked at the Level One stage that we are about to start. But they recur throughout the Ends domain. For example, think of a school system in which the board addresses what skills and insights are to be attained by young persons of a particular geographic area for a tax burden of a certain amount. In that same system, a classroom teacher is faced with deciding what skill level should be attained by little Jan by this afternoon and whether that is worth letting a few other children wait awhile.

So let's begin our work by looking for the results component at the highest level of ends. We suggest starting the Ends development process by naming "candidates" for the largest Ends policy, which we call E #1. To begin, ponder questions like these: If this organization were to disappear from the face of the earth tomorrow, why would we put it back? What are we buying with (or what justifies) the resources consumed by this organization every year?

What does our ownership demand from this organization? Remember you are concerning yourselves with what the organization is for, not what it does.

This is a brainstorming exercise, so it would be helpful for someone to record on a flip chart the various suggestions as they emerge from board members. Pay no attention to your existing mission statement except as its content comes up naturally during the brainstorming. Press for full participation, encouraging the various differences in emphasis or values held by your board members to be represented.

We use examples from a mental health center board, but you will see that there are obvious parallels with other nonprofit or public organizations. We assume that your board has just produced a list like that to follow. (The items are the sort that commonly show up at this point in the process.) Remember, we are looking for what results this organization exists to produce. What is this organization for?

The following are brainstormed "candidates" for the Level One Ends policy. The question: What is our organization for?

Offer quality programs and services
Support parents of mentally ill people
Help mentally ill people
Help people reach their potential
Marriage counseling
Jobs
Advocate for the mentally ill
Make life enjoyable for low-functioning people
Responsible use of resources
Community support
Assist families in solving problems

When engaged in this exercise, continue the process until a dozen or so phrases are on the list or as long as the contributions keep coming, whichever is longer. As in any brainstorming, it is best if you do not stop to judge or even discuss any one of the suggestions. Just keep adding to the list until a natural stopping point is reached. Having collected these candidates for top billing, review them. A certain amount of weeding out will be required. It will be helpful if you have a brief discussion aimed at reducing the pride of authorship some board members might feel, for everyone will be invited to be brutal in critiquing the list. We illustrate by critiquing our own:

- We begin by eliminating the words that describe good intentions or effort rather than results. Examples from our list include the words *support, assist,* and *advocate.* They bespeak not the attainment of anything but commitment and intention. They can be fulfilled while having absolutely no effect upon consumers. Be tough; allow yourselves and your CEO no points for supporting, assisting, or advocating; rather, hold yourselves to the discipline of requiring results for people. Your staff will no doubt have to support and assist and advocate, but these are means and have no value apart from the benefits they produce. Do not inappropriately dignify these efforts as Ends. *Your organization does not exist to try.*

- Now, we go beyond effort words and eliminate means of all types from the list. Even the most Ends-conscious board will find that it has produced some. Our list contains several. Programs and services, even high-quality ones, are means, not ends. (Actually, their quality can only be determined in relation to their ability to produce the Ends. So, apart from their achievement of Ends, how would we know they are high quality?) That resources be used responsibly is important but is not an ends issue, as it fails to identify even one of the three components of ends. Helping mentally ill people, while broadly identifying the recipients of intended results, does not state the outcome or result those recipients should expect to receive; helping per se is an activity (means). Marriage counseling is likewise an activity. Be suspicious of verbs (help, offer). If they describe your organization's actions rather than the benefit to be received by the consumer, they signify means. *Teaching* children to read is means; children *can read* is ends.

- We eliminate or clarify the candidate statements that are ambiguous as to their ends or means identity. Notice that on our list, *jobs* and *community support* could be ends or means. If the board is remarking on the fact that the organization employs people, this is a means issue and should be discarded from the list. If the board intends, on the other hand, that certain consumers should be employed as a result of the organization's efforts, this is an ends issue. Likewise, community support could mean that the board wishes the community to be supportive of the organization. This is a means issue. If the board intends that it wants to see a difference in the ability of clients to integrate into the community, or in the ability of the community to include clients in everyday life, these are ends issues and should stay on the list. *Education* is a similar word; if it means the state of being educated, it is a result. If it means the process of education, it is a means. Beware of words that can go either way. It is so easy to get off-track in working with Ends that we strongly caution you not to put even one foot on the slippery slope.

Let's see what a revised version of our list may look like, along with brief comments about the reason for revising.

Candidate Statement	Comment
Offer quality programs and services	Entirely means
Support parents of mentally ill people	Recipients are defined but no results; support is means
Help mentally ill people	Recipients are defined but no results; help is means
Help people reach their potential	That people reach their potential is a result; helping, however, is a means
Marriage counseling	Entirely means
Jobs	Ambiguous; could be ends or means
Advocate for the mentally ill	Recipients are defined but no results; advocate is means
Make life enjoyable for low-functioning people	Very close; if "life (is) enjoyable . . ." then results and recipients are defined

Responsible use of resources	Entirely means
Community support	Ambiguous; could be ends or means
Assist families in solving problems	Means if the focus is our assisting; if "families solve problems," then a result and recipients are defined

Our revised list shows that the elimination of means statements, including "effort words," and the identification of ambiguous statements change the picture considerably. As you can tell, we are bending over backward to weed out anything that isn't strictly a result. We haven't argued with the vagueness of stated results, but we have been brutal on means masquerading as results. We know that such care may seem to be overkill. But keep in mind that the top-level statement sets the stage for all further Ends work. If we cannot observe the simple principles at this global level, how can we hope to observe them as we go into more detail and potentially more complexity? Since subsequent Ends work further defines the global intention, putting the wrong elements into the global statements destines further work to define the wrong things. That is exactly what boards customarily do; they waste a great deal of time working on the wrong questions.

At this point, your board should make a new list. Now that the board is prepared to be more rigorous about the results component, you may be able to add in the recipients component as you move ahead. If you find it necessary to stick to the results part even longer, do so. It is better to have an extra step than to take a chance on forsaking rigor.

So far, we have identified that the parents of mentally ill people may be recipients of undefined results produced by the organization. What should the results be? Does the board want to prescribe that parents of mentally ill persons get an occasional rest? Does it want them to acquire certain skills? Does it want them to achieve a level of psychological comfort? Suppose the board has massaged these points and produced new candidates for the top Ends statement that look like this:

- Parents of mentally ill people will have an occasional rest.
- Mentally ill people will achieve life skills consistent with their abilities.

- Mentally ill people will have the opportunity to fulfill their potential.
- Mentally ill people will have job skills or jobs.
- Public policy and community standards will be accepting of the mentally ill.
- Chronically mentally ill people will have the ability to enjoy their life.
- Families will have the ability to solve problems without violence.

If you've moved along like our example board, it looks as if you have identified results and recipients. (Don't worry even yet about the cost component; we will attend to it in a little while.) Now examine the items on the list for their level of ambition. To hold yourself accountable for mentally ill people having the *opportunity* to meet their potential is less ambitious than being accountable for their actually meeting it. What if your staff produced a great deal of opportunity, but no one reached potential (remember, the CEO gets to use any reasonable interpretation of that word)? Would that be OK? Likewise, being accountable for people having job skills is less ambitious than being accountable for their having jobs. Which level of ambition is appropriate? Try to be as ambitious as is still doable.

At this point, you will notice that you have created an incomplete list of results and recipients, none of which by itself constitutes the broadest level of Ends policy, Policy E #1. Our list contains Ends statements that may be important to include at further levels of definition. But the largest Ends statement must encompass all other statements in this category. Said another way, if you are relatively certain about these less-than-global designations of results and recipients, then the eventual global statement must encompass all of these and possibly more.

Upon inspection, your board's list, as does this one, may fall into some identifiable areas or themes. Our list seems to fall into three areas: mentally ill individuals and their parents, families with emotional or adjustment difficulties, and the general public (its policy or point of view). What is needed is a statement that encloses these lower-level themes.

Here is an attempt at such a statement: *People with psychiatric and emotional problems will achieve their potential in a caring community.*

We make no attempt to defend this sample Ends policy, since reasonable people on a board, in different situations, may decide very differently. We simply offer it as an example for discussion.

We will not discard the list we labored over, even though it has yielded its most important contribution: helping us conceive of a global statement. Sometimes the original list has within it the global statement; that may be your experience. But be ready to extrapolate if you need to, as we just did. In any event, the list that is left will be used later when we consider expanding our Ends to Level Two.

But to round out our tentative global statement (E #1), let's now add the cost element. Remember the intent of cost as an ends concept in Policy Governance is to declare what some result is worth, or how much of the result we want for the money or other cost entailed. That can be expressed in different ways: an exact monetary amount, a relative priority among other results, or an external comparative statement. In the case of government, the cost of results can even be citizen freedoms curtailed, as well as taxes and user fees imposed. For example, safe motor vehicle flow is at the cost, in part, of loss of freedom to drive at my own chosen speed. A federation may produce for its members a recognizable symbol of quality (logo, service mark, or accreditation) at the cost of their giving up some autonomy of action.

At this topmost level in our exercise, we will use an external comparison, possibly the easiest to use at this level. The kind of external comparison will be "market," the average amount of good that would ordinarily be possible for whatever amount of money is expended. In other words, the efficiency (results per cost) should be about what others can do. This is a useful comparison in that it works even with changes in budget size, and it affirms that we want to do at least an average job of producing desired effects for the money being spent. Taking that path, the Ends Policy E #1 in its entirety might be worded thus:

Policy E #1: Global Ends Policy

People with psychiatric and emotional problems will achieve their potential in a caring community with a level of efficiency comparable to similar organizations.

This Level One Ends policy appears on the circle diagram as depicted in Figure 7.2.

Figure 7.2. Ends, Level One.

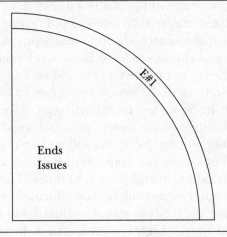

Note: The global or mega-Ends statement, shown in the upper right-hand quadrant, encloses or forms the base for all further Ends decisions.

Your board would undoubtedly argue several aspects of the foregoing E #1 policy. For example, someone would say that producing at the average is not ambitious enough, that the wording should be, say, "at an efficiency materially beyond the median." Another will argue with the word *potential,* preferring that the statement reflect an external instead of internal reference point like "will achieve a substantially normal life." And still others will argue other issues. This is as it should be. Also, the board would be gathering information so as not to come up with an undoable dream. Remember, Ends may flow from your dreams, but they are meant to be practical tools in directing the organization.

So the E #1 policy, only somewhat like what is traditionally meant by "mission," will be characterized as follows:

- Brief, but including all three ends components
- Doable, not merely a wish or unattainable goal
- Clear, but not having to bear the burden of being snappy like a slogan
- Expansive enough to embrace the fullness of your intent
- Narrow enough to distinguish your organization from the larger world

Take another look at the E #1 statement we have produced. Even though the board will probably choose to define the words further in E #2 and maybe E #3 levels of policy, the purpose of the organization is quite succinctly and clearly put as the statement stands. If the board chooses to leave Ends development at this level without further expansion, the CEO would set out to construct his or her own definitions of the words, undoubtedly taking great care in doing so, for the board will be expecting a convincing argument that reasonable interpretations are being achieved. On the other hand, the CEO knows that he or she will receive no credit for well-designed programs, busy and competent staff, low costs-per-client-visit, staff-client ratios, or full work schedules. The board will no longer mistake such means for Ends performance. In fact, if the CEO can achieve the Ends as stated in this global statement with no professional staff, a high cost-per-visit, or by waving a magic wand, the board will be happy.

As an aside, if we *really* want to harness innovation and creativity to the public's benefit in health care, education, municipal government, and other public services, *this is exactly the way our governing boards must behave.* Not doing so—staying stuck in the traditional mode—is a travesty imposing a massive toll in human and material cost.

Before we move on from the creation of the top level of Ends, let us look at some first-level Ends statements in various types of organizations.

City Government

The City of Greattown will be a community in which people can live, work, and visit safely and profitably for a tax rate of no greater than cities of comparable size in this state.

Professional Association

Members of the National Association of Policy Governance Boards will have the skills and knowledge to govern responsibly in an environment supportive of real accountability for an annual membership fee of $1,200.

Hospital/Health Care System

The purpose of Healing Health System is a maximally healthy population for total expenditures of $320 million.

Research Institution

The Hangnail Research Institute will produce knowledge necessary for a life without the pain of hangnails for a cost of no more than $18 million per annum.

ASSIGNMENT: Examine the E #1 policy that your board has developed. Check to see that it really is an Ends statement, that it contains no means, and that it is the most general yet doable statement of what your organization is for. Then ask yourself if your board would be willing to accept any reasonable interpretation the CEO chooses to give the words of that policy. If the board is willing to do so, it need say no more about Ends. If it cannot, it must go to the next level, Level Two.

Here's a Little More Detail: Going to Level Two

Moving to the next level involves defining which aspects of the higher-level policy the board wishes to control further than the "any reasonable interpretation" control it already has. If the Level One policy is crafted well, this will mostly involve the further definition of what is already contained in it. Let's return to our mental health center example.

Policy E#1 states: *People with psychiatric and emotional problems will achieve their potential in a caring community with a level of efficiency comparable to similar organizations.* What components of this statement can the board further define? Clearly, there are a number of words in the Level One policy that are open to a great deal of interpretation. Which people are we referring to? Do we mean old or young people, rich or poor people, urban or rural people, members of families or single people? All of these categories? In what proportions? What sorts of psychiatric or emotional problems do we mean? Mild ones, severe ones, those that lead to criminal behavior, intermittently disabling ones? Indeed, just what constitutes a psychiatric or emotional problem? Who hasn't had an emotional "problem" of some sort?

And what does it mean to achieve one's potential? Is that everything one is capable of or everything one desires? Is potential measured in life satisfaction or in economic achievement? Is this potential as perceived by experts, by affected persons, or by their families, friends, or employers? And which community or communities do we mean? Local, regional, or national communities, communities of similarly troubled people, church communities, the community at large?

Are the various results that could be contained in the broad statement equally important in terms of access to our resources? If not equally important, then what are the various relative importances? Are the various recipient groups equally important? Could the CEO target one specific subset of people with psychiatric problems, or must the CEO be sure to cover a representative group of all types?

And just what does *efficiency* mean? Cost for results can be the same when we accomplish a lot for a few or a little for many. Do we mean efficiency in terms of the organization's cost alone, or does it include the cost to recipients (for example, user fees or consumers' personal costs in getting to the organization) as well? And just what constitute comparable organizations? In our community, our state or province, our country? Of our size, type of staff, organizational maturity?

Make no mistake, *every one of these questions will be answered,* because they *must* be answered in the process of operation. True, they may not be answered in words and may not be answered consciously, but things will turn out one way or another along all these dimensions purely as a function of operating. The board does not have to answer them, but if it does not, it is duty bound to accept the way the answers come out (either by CEO-staff choice or by default) as long as a reasonable interpretation of the global statement is honored. The board, then, has first opportunity to provide the general answers that will control further definitions made by the CEO.

In our example, let us suppose that the board has given further definition to its Level One policy by the four Level Two policies that follow. Again, Policy E #1 states: *People with psychiatric and emotional problems will achieve their potential in a caring community with a level of efficiency comparable to similar organizations.* Moving to Level Two might have this result:

Policy E #2a   Independent Living

Chronically ill or disabled persons achieve a level of independence commensurate with their circumstances at a cost of 55 percent of all resources.

Policy E #2b   Public Policy

A public policy environment supportive of the particular needs of low- or intermittently functioning people, for a cost not to exceed 10 percent of all resources.

Policy E #2c   Work and Family

Adult persons with emotional or family problems achieve enhanced family and occupational functioning at a cost not to exceed 25 percent of all resources.

Policy E #2d   School Readiness

Emotionally disturbed children gain the ability to utilize educational resources in the general community at a cost not to exceed 10 percent of all resources.

We assume that the board spent some time discovering the extent of the need in the community and listening to the input of the various parties in the ownership who would have an opinion about the board's choices. In many communities the example given above would be indefensible, in light of the demographics and the other resources in the community. In other communities our example might be appropriate. In any event, our purpose is not to suggest what the Ends should be but to offer an example of their framing. Each board will develop its own unique method of controlling the organizational Ends.

You will have noticed in this example that the board has stated its estimation of the worth of each result area from the standpoint of the use of available resources. It is obvious in this illustration that cost and relative priority are virtually the same issue. But this is only one approach to cost or worth that may make sense to the board. If a board can only agree on a statement that one result is to have the "dominant priority," then that is what it should say. We are not recommending that the board say this but simply stating that the board must say what it feels. And if *dominant priority* captures it best, then those are the words to be used. Are they meaningless? Absolutely not. The CEO would then set out to abide by an interpretation that he or she can later justify to the board as a reasonable interpretation of this broad term.

One board of our acquaintance made the "market penetration" in various need areas constant across all results. That is, if available funds and methods were capable of reaching 25 percent of the need in each area, OK. If they made it possible, due to better methods or more funds, to reach 45 percent of the need in each area, OK. In any case, the CEO would be called upon to demonstrate that at least commonly accepted efficiency was met, but the results would be spread across the various result areas (or it could have been across various recipient classifications with the same result) in the way prescribed. It is not our intention to dictate that there is only one manner in which the cost or relative worth of the many possible organizational results can be expressed. Only your creativity limits the ways the board can express relative priority or cost of the results it wants.

Take this a step further. Consider that the board might want to control the proportions of results that require expending its scarce resources but is willing to let results that pay for themselves go uncontrolled. In other words, the organization has some funding base that allows it to subsidize certain results, that is, to offer them at no cost to the recipient or at a cost below the cost of production. While carefully husbanding those scarce subsidy funds, the board in our illustration feels no need to limit what the CEO can accomplish when providing results that are paid for in full by the recipients. The board can express its priorities, then, with respect to use of subsidy money, enabling the CEO to do as much as he or she wishes and can arrange beyond the use of subsidy. The only control over the self-financing results is that they must be a reasonable interpretation of the E #1 policy. As we said, there is no end to possibilities.

As you examine your Level One policy and go further into Level Two, allow yourself to re-examine Level One from time to time. Sometimes you will find that the experience of going into Level Two informs your wisdom in such a way that another iteration of Level One is in order. If you find that at Level Two you are developing more than a handful of policies, there is a good chance you are jumping levels, going into too much detail too soon. You may frame your Level Two policies around the "which people" aspects of Ends, or around the "what benefit" aspects, or you may decide to use both aspects. The choice is absolutely yours, and you can be as creative as you wish, as long as you use ends terminology and move into detail one level at a time.

As in the other policy categories, each Level Two policy can be further defined by the board, if the board is not willing to accept any reasonable interpretation of some part of Level Two by the CEO. The board that decides to further define at this level will simply take the words of Level Two policies as a starting point and proceed to define them. Thus, one of the further definitions of Policy E #2a, *Chronically ill or disabled persons will achieve a level of independence commensurate with their circumstances at a cost of 55 percent of resources,* could be as follows:

Policy E #3a   Independent Living: Level Three

Occupational independence is a priority result area for chronically but moderately ill persons, while for severely ill persons, the acquisition of basic life skills will be the priority result to be achieved.

Your board should engage in similar further definition using its Level Two policies as starting points. As in previous policy categories, the board can then decide to further define its newly created Level Three policies. As always, the board defines its own words until it can accept any reasonable interpretation from the CEO.

The Level Two Ends policies, in addition to the policy E #3a just added, increase the board's definitional control of Ends as illustrated in Figure 7.3.

The exercise we have just described is likely to pose as many questions as it answers with regard to the Ends demands that your board should make on the CEO. It is to be expected that your board may not be sure of just what is reasonable to expect of the CEO in terms of results for consumers, or who all the possible consumers are. The board may not know what future need is likely to be or how it may change. Your board inevitably will need to arrange for education and owner and consumer consultation in order to collect the information it requires to make good Ends decisions. This education is so important that we can easily conceive of over half the board's time being spent in its pursuit.

You have probably noticed that there are more potential consumers of the benefits to be produced by your organization than there are resources to go around. This puts the board squarely in

Figure 7.3. Ends Policies Completed.

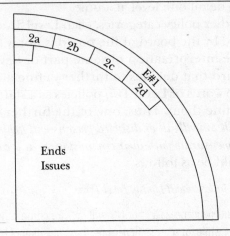

Note: Ends policies, as illustrated in the text, now extend from the outside edge of the policy circle (the broadest level) into varying depths, depending on the board's need to make further definitions before turning Ends over to the CEO.

the position of deciding the distribution of a scarce commodity, that is, organizational outputs. This is not an easy position to be in, but one for which a board representing the owners is truly required. This is why a board exists—to carry out this crucial ownership function that, as the organization develops, is truly definitive. Your job is to create the future.

At this point, take a look at where we've come in the mental health example. Admittedly, the Ends policy depth is not great. There is not a lot of detail, and much latitude has been left to the CEO to make decisions about just what results will be received by just which subpopulations, and at what cost those results will be produced. But policy making at only the depth shown has given this hypothetical board greater control over the real impact of their organization than most boards ever dream of. Even a two-level Ends control by the board expresses monumentally more governance leadership than many times this amount of involvement in how the staff operates. Specifying Ends even broadly is like telling the taxi driver your destination in a few words rather than backseat driving with volumes.

Next Chapter

This chapter completes Part Two, in which we have described the process of developing policies in the Policy Governance mode. We have found policies in the Executive Limitations, Governance Process, and Board-CEO Linkage categories to be quite stable. You will undoubtedly need to adjust them from time to time, but if you have created your set of policies attending closely to Policy Governance principles and to your own values, the ones you have now will likely be with you for years. Ends policies are more likely to undergo regular review and updating.

In Chapter Eight we discuss the board's documents. The "voice" of governance is enhanced in Policy Governance inasmuch as board instructions, philosophy, and intentions are clearly its own, not mere reflections of what a staff has put together. Consequently, those instruments that document what the board says take on a different look, or at least a new significance.

Ready, Steady, Go

Part Three deals with creating and maintaining a Policy Governance culture. When a board makes the change from traditional governance—even competently done traditional governance—the board room is never the same again. In fact, the word *transformation* comes closer to describing the shift. Having created the policies illustrated thus far certainly sets the stage. But there is further important work yet to come!

Chapter Eight

The Board's Documents

Your board's implementation of Policy Governance will cause a radical change in the way it defines and does its job. It should expect its documents to change, too. In this chapter, we examine with you the various documents that belong to the board or that describe or affect the board's job.

At the outset, let us emphasize a major board document difference between Policy Governance and governance as we have known it. We are accustomed to omnibus documents, ones that belong, more or less, to the entire organization. Policy Governance makes it possible to accurately describe certain documents as belonging to the board. Traditionally, we have become accustomed to seeing materials whose ownership is either unclear or feigned. We know these documents belong to the organization, but we do not know to which authority in the organization. To outsiders, this more specific knowledge is unimportant; it matters only that an action is taken by the organization. Were the clinic hours set by the board, the CEO, or the clinic director? As a patient, it doesn't matter. Was the stop sign placed by the city council, city manager, or department of public works? As a driver, it doesn't matter. In any event, the governing body is accountable.

For proper interrelationships of the organization's parts, however, it is crucial to know who is saying or deciding what. Yet we are used to plans that have been worked on by both board and staff. We see budgets and internal procedures put together by staff but not official until a board action has been taken and staff recommendations, upon board blessing, are transformed into board policy. It is difficult, if not impossible, in the traditional system to identify just *whose document* anything actually is! It is even common for traditional boards to speak with pride of joint documents and board-staff teamwork, as if obscuring authorship and authority were what teamwork is about. Policy Governance boards know that some of the documents in their organizations are theirs, and some are not. They are not misled by the disempowering tenet that decisions aren't official until the board says they are, a doctrine based on a weak notion of delegation.

In this chapter, we examine three major document types that belong to the board *alone*. These documents are *bylaws, minutes,* and *policies* (in some cases, bylaws belong to and are controlled by a general membership). All other documents belong to the CEO or other staff (for which the board would hold the CEO accountable). First, we look at your organization's bylaws, commenting on aspects of bylaws that affect and sometimes can impede good governance. Then we suggest some ways in which your board can make its minutes an efficient and useful record of its proceedings. Last, we discuss the manner in which it can establish and maintain its policy manual so that governing policies are up-to-date and accessible. We do not look at the documents generated by the CEO under the authority delegated to him or her, for properly authorized CEO decisions do not have to be reiterated by the board to be official. Hence staff materials are not board materials but are fully as official.

The Hierarchy of Documents

We find it useful to view board documents as a hierarchy, each level in the hierarchy having its own purpose. At the top-most level in the hierarchy is one to which we refer only briefly. This is the document that established the organization that your board governs. The Articles of Incorporation, Letters Patent, or legislation under which your organization was established created an "artificial person," an empty shell, an entity that started to exist and have abilities such as to bank, borrow, employ, and have certain engagements with the world in which it is situated. The language of this founding document is usually general, for its purpose is simply to establish an organization that has legal status. This document belongs to neither the board nor the CEO but to the governmental authority that issued it. We do not consider this document, since it is common for it to be written in such general language that the governance process is not affected.

At the next level in the document hierarchy are the bylaws. Legislation-based organizations typically have no bylaws, whereas nonprofits consistently have them. The reason is that statutes often spell out the provisions that would have been contained in bylaws. If there are bylaws, they normally belong to a "membership," a group under nonprofit law comparable to stockholders in an equity corporation. In a true membership organization such as a trade or professional association, this legal membership is the same as the ownership concept in Policy Governance. In nonprofits that are not true membership associations (such as a local social service agency), the concept of membership is relatively meaningless. It frequently is nothing more than a public relations or fund-raising mechanism, bearing no relation to the Policy Governance ownership concept at all. In order to comply with the legal requirement to name a membership and yet to avoid the sham of a meaningless membership, some nonprofits have simply constituted the board itself as the membership. The added benefit in some instances is that the board protects itself from the potential for membership factions to hijack the board. We find it regrettable when boards protect themselves from the diversity of their true ownerships, though we do sympathize with boards' needs to protect their process from counterfeit ownerships. We note, however, that any board (even a very large, "representative" board) is itself a pseudo-ownership. This is why Policy Governance makes much of the need for boards to consult widely outside themselves.

Bylaws exist merely to take the empty shell created by law and describe the manner in which it can take on life. Hence the bylaws serve to describe the membership of the new entity and to set out how that membership can elect or appoint the board, as well as how to change or remove board members. The rules about annual or membership meetings, notice, quorum, and board demographics serve this purpose. The bylaws also describe under what circumstances the board can be said to have spoken. Normally, bylaws establish that a board has spoken upon a majority vote at a properly noticed meeting where a quorum is present. Thus the organization has moved from a paper entity to one in which real-life decisions can be made. It has not yet spoken but is now capable of speech.

Minutes form the next level of board documents, and they exist to be a legal record of the board's meetings and actions. The empty shell—the artificial person created by Articles of Incorporation, Letters Patent, or legislation—speaks, and its decisions are recorded in official form.

The final level of the document hierarchy in Policy Governance is the board's policies. (In traditional governance, the hierarchy at this point splits into approvals, positions, and a variety of unconnected and scattergun pronouncements.) Board policies in Policy Governance constitute the complete registry of what the artificial person has spoken. In Policy Governance boards, the only pronouncements of the board are policies formulated according to the model's principles. If your board has been working through this book, it has probably completed its board and staff means policies and is working on its Ends policies. You are nearing completion (for the time being, for it is never really finished) of a complete set of board pronouncements.

Before we embark on a discussion of the three types of documents that appear in our hierarchy below the initiating Articles, Letters, or legislation, let us reiterate that once the bylaws have established the organization's governing structure, the *only* pronouncements made by the board are the policies. This has major implications for your governance transition. It means that any documents the board viewed as wholly or partially its own before implementing Policy Governance cease to be board documents and may cease to exist altogether. Hence, the budget, strategic plan, long-term goals, pre–Policy Governance policy manual or any other pre–Policy Governance documents should be handed over to the CEO. The CEO is likely to find many of these documents helpful, so they are not wasted. Conversely, the CEO may abandon or change any of them, since he or she has the right, as you will remember from policy BCL #3c, to make all further decisions and policies that follow from board pronouncements about Ends and Executive Limitations.

It is understandable that you might feel "stripped bare" by the thought of relinquishing your hold on these familiar documents. Consider, though, that the need to control them directly no longer exists if your board's own policies are complete, and your monitoring is in effect. Consider also that the board's previous "control" of staff actions through document approvals was either over-control (of details and prescribed means) or under-control (of Ends and limits on means), an illusory control at best. Moreover, such board involvement in these traditional documents necessarily drew the board into staff material. We sympathize with any discomfort you might have when declaring, in effect, that budgets, long-range plans, personnel policies, and other traditional documents are not governance documents at all, but management documents.

Three Steps in Governance Documentation

In this section, we are going to examine in detail bylaws, minutes, and the policy manual. Since these are legitimately governance rather than management documents, it is important that your board maintain direct control over them, that the documents themselves be model-consistent, and that they are kept current.

The Bylaws

Some organizations have both a constitution and bylaws. We are not aware of any purpose served by this duality. They are indistinguishable in their purpose, and for brevity we refer to *bylaws* as a generic term embracing all the components that might appear in both.

As we have noted, bylaws are the documents that spell out the arrangements and conditions under which an artificial person can speak. Your bylaws should contain a description of the manner in which people can join or have standing in your organization (other than at the staff level). This may be a description of the organization's ownership, or it may be the identification of a smaller group than the total ownership. It may identify the group commonly known as the membership. There should also be a description of how often and under what conditions of notice the persons with standing may elect or appoint a board to speak on behalf of the total group.

One of the features of Policy Governance is its insistence that documents and decisions belong to *somebody* (or some *body*, like the board). We have made that point in discarding the familiar omnibus documents created by staff and approved, blessed, and embraced by the board (such as budgets and program plans). We replace such documents with policy documents specific to the board, complemented by separate documents and decisions that clearly belong to the CEO and staff.

Now let us extend the same reasoning to the bylaws, a consideration that seems to have escaped traditional governance. Bylaws are a document. A document is merely a set of decisions about some identifiable topic. Whose decisions are they, and who has the right to change them? In many cases, the bylaws belong to the board because the board is tantamount to the broader membership. But in true membership associations, the bylaws should belong to the membership, which has the right to use the bylaws to control the board that operates in its service. Either the board owns the bylaws or the membership does. In other words, bylaws should not belong to the membership *and* the board, with each putting in its chosen list of provisions.

We realize that a membership, when large, has a hard time truly making any decisions that are its own. Boards and other mechanisms steer the membership to a large degree. But we would argue that whether or not the membership makes its decisions seriously and assertively, its prerogatives are still its prerogatives. So we treat the bylaws in membership organizations as truly a document of the members. In city government, the parallel document is often called a city charter, which is passed by voters in a referendum and is, therefore, a document of the owners, not of the city council.

So where are we going with this analysis? Simply to this: if there is a real membership, it owns the bylaws and must establish them to control and empower the board that will represent it. Just as between board and staff, the membership should not dictate the means of the board, and the board should not assume prerogatives rightly belonging to the members. When a membership declares that it gives its official voice to a majority (criterion vote) of a certain group (the board) when a certain number of that group is present (quorum requirement), it is establishing what voice will officially be its voice in the governing setting. But to go further and tell that board, for example, what committees to have or how to have checks signed is to prescribe that board's means. Why saddle the board with prescribed methods when the membership can more effectively charge the board with a required product?

Of course when there is no separate membership, the board is on its own and must own the bylaws itself. As we describe features of the bylaws that affect the practice of governance, we refer to both situations. We do not address all possible aspects of bylaws (such as type of notice or whether telephone meetings can be held) but only those with a substantive impact on the quality of governance.

Board size: There is no one right number for board size, but try to keep the board small! The bigger the board, the less likely it is to be business-like and disciplined. Have a good reason if you want to make it bigger than seven. If you are an eight-county board, you probably have a good reason. If you want to be representative, remember that you cannot be big enough to represent the diversity of the ownership unless, of course, the ownership is very small. Strategies of obtaining outside input to an effective board can ensure that large numbers of people have a voice more surely than expanding the board to an inefficient size.

Attendance: We commonly see bylaws that state that a board member who "without excuse" misses a criterion number of meetings "may" be asked to resign. Such an attendance provision is ineffective. All absences tend to qualify as "excused" if the board member phones to say he or she will be unable to attend. Hence the normal attendance provision has been effective in eliciting courtesy, not attendance. Further, the words "may be asked to resign" are permissive. They require that the board take a definite action to remove someone. This is socially awkward to do, and therefore is seldom done. We recommend wording such as, "A member who fails to attend 75 percent of all board meetings in a year [or three meetings in a row, or four meetings in any consecutive twelve-month period] will be deemed to have resigned." This can be softened somewhat by adding that a member may be reinstated at his or her request, but only once in a term. If yours is an appointed board, change the words to indicate that the appointing authority will be asked to replace a delinquent board member.

Our recommendation is not intended to be punitive. There is nothing morally bad about being too busy to serve on a board. We simply recommend that boards not hinder their own performance by allowing seats to be taken up by nonattenders. The board has a job to do. No one would think of applying for a job for which they were too busy to show up. We are completely unmoved by appeals for leniency on the grounds that board members are volunteers. The paid or unpaid status of board members is irrelevant to the importance of the job. Moreover, the persons most hurt by nonattendance are other volunteers, the ones who go to the trouble to attend regularly.

Quorum: We have seen bylaws that set out quorum requirements that are laughably low, sometimes as low as one-third or even one-fourth, serving only to indicate that attendance doesn't matter. Quorum requirements that are below 50 percent make it possible that from one meeting to the next, the organization can be governed by *entirely different groups of people!* This hardly protects continuity and board wholeness. We suggest that you establish quorum at no less than 60 percent.

Passing vote: Your bylaws should be clear about what constitutes a passing vote. It is usual to see that a simple majority is the standard, but some boards differ from this. If your board is planning to operate in a consensus mode, define the word *consensus!* We have seen the word mean that every board member must agree with a proposition before it is accepted by the board. We have also seen it mean that the board will strive to ensure that no one is silenced and that all may speak, or that the manner of deliberating will be pleasant and aimed at arriving at compromise. We point out to our clients that even if they are using the strictest definition of *consensus* (that all must agree), this is still voting. The number of votes required to defeat a proposition is just one.

Officers: Your bylaws should identify the officers required by law. Because minimalism will serve you well, don't have more than the legal minimum unless there is truly an officer job crying out for attention. We rarely find that to be the case. In many jurisdictions, boards are required only to have a chair and a secretary. Settle for these two until experience dictates that more are needed.

Be careful not to describe these positions in a way that complicates or invalidates your delegation to the CEO. We often see bylaws that state that the chair *is* the CEO. This may be stated directly, or it may be indirect. Wording such as "the chair shall have general supervision of the affairs of the organization" or "the executive director shall report to the board through the chair" are indirect statements that the chair, not the executive director, is the CEO. Avoid such words unless you really intend the chair to be personally accountable to the board for organizational performance.

Remember that if you want your chief staff officer to play that crucial CEO role for you, the board chair will not have accountability for, or authority over, organizational performance. That burden falls to the CEO, who is accountable to the board rather than to the chair. The only reason for the position of chair to exist is that the board needs a "first among equals" to help it maintain the discipline of its own job. The chair is the board's servant and leader in one, but only with respect to the board's job, not with respect to the CEO's. Bylaws wording should reflect this role.

Describe the secretary as accountable for the accuracy of board documents. This is probably all that needs to be said about this position. Being secretary may have nothing to do with taking minutes, but it will have a lot to do with certifying the integrity of minutes and other board documents. Given that in Policy Governance the board has its own documents, the role of secretary becomes more important than is customary. In the policy form we show later, notice that the secretary attests to the board's adoption of the policy.

If you have a CEO, you do not need a treasurer, especially since the accountability of this position tends to directly overlap with the accountability of the CEO. Holding a treasurer responsible for books of accounts, disbursements, and receipts cannot be legitimate while holding the CEO accountable for the same things. Having a board treasurer in organizations with a CEO is a mindless holdover from smaller, non-CEO organizations.

Committees: There is no need for any committees to be established in the bylaws, unless they are committees of the membership in those cases wherein the membership and ownership are synonymous and, therefore, where the membership owns the bylaws. If that is the case, the membership's dictating what committees the board will have is an example of prescribing means to a subordinate body and should be avoided. Of course, if the bylaws belong to the board, then the board has a right to establish its committees there. But we recommend against it. Board committees can and should, if necessary, be established by the board in policy. When your board creates committees, it will have more control over its own governance by avoiding bylaws-based committees. Because bylaws are a less changeable document than policies, describing board committees there creates a less fluid arrangement. Of course at this stage in our text, it may go without saying that staff committees would not be established by the board at all.

Still another common committee phenomenon is unique to membership organizations and local governments. Sometimes boards create committees of members in order to get them involved in organizational work, to take advantage of a free source of labor, to co-opt membership decisions (by involving a few members to begin with), or to provide a venue to observe potential leaders. While there would be nothing dysfunctional about such groups if they were employed by the board only to help with governance tasks, they are commonly and unfortunately engaged in staff work. While there would be nothing dysfunctional about their being involved in staff work if the staff were controlling the process, these committees by definition are foisted on the staff by the board.

This practice can be as complicated as it is dysfunctional. Such committees often become power bases for certain members, who are then reluctant to give up the role, even if the board or staff think the job no longer is needed. These committees are very difficult to "uncreate," due to the political fallout. In city government, the council might establish a number of citizen boards and commissions (for example, parks and recreation). In this case, is the commission to advise or govern staff about that topic, or is it to advise the council about citizen needs for parks and recreation? These questions are almost never answered clearly, leaving a tangle of organizational design that is quite difficult to undo. But the political tides are just as strong in membership associations as in the real political arena.

Be cognizant of this phenomenon as you deliberate the adoption of Policy Governance, for its adoption will almost certainly cause you to discontinue some committees. Although different circumstances call for different strategies, the most common strategy for us to suggest is for the board to tackle the changes all at once. While everyone is geared up for change, multiple changes are often easier. Stringing the changes out in order to soften the blow can be like getting into the pool one toe at a time.

At any rate, avoid making similar problems as your legacy for your successor boards! The aim of governance is not to see how many moving parts you can design. Some of those unnecessary parts take on a life of their own! It is hard to drive efficiently to your destination if a large part of your organizational effort is consumed by unendingly tending to dysfunctional parts.

CEO: Describe your CEO's job and the delegation you will make to him or her in your policies, not in the bylaws. Naturally the bylaws would not deal with insurance, borrowing, check signing, purchasing, investing, and other staff means issues. The exception is if the membership wishes to restrict the range of board latitude (thence the range that the board can delegate to the CEO) on such matters. Whatever the board has the right to control is best done in its policies.

As you can see, we recommend keeping bylaws very lean. Put nothing in them except what really needs to be there. So when your board reviews its bylaws, it should

- Remember that bylaws are often harder to change than policies. It increases your flexibility to keep as much as possible in policies, not bylaws.
- Acknowledge the importance of the board's job by requiring regular attendance.
- Set quorum of at least 60 percent.
- Establish at least majority vote to qualify as a board decision.
- Remove any language that appears to assign staff jobs to officers. Make sure that the chair is not described directly or indirectly as the CEO, unless you really mean the chair to have this role and accountability.
- If you have a CEO, eliminate the treasurer position.
- Remove all language about committees except, where applicable, for committees established by the membership for its own use.
- Remove provisions that deal with the CEO's job.
- Remove provisions that deal with staff means.

Minutes

Board minutes are simply a legal record of the board's meetings, actions, and decisions. In Policy Governance, a board's actions, or words, are a group product. Individual statements, actions, points of view, and preferences, while they may be important preliminaries to a board decision, are not official board matters and thus do not need to be recorded as part of the board's proceedings. Hence, narrative minutes of the "he said, she said" variety are unnecessary and usually a wasteful expense.

We do not need to tell you how time-consuming and frustrating it can be to both write and read narrative minutes. Boards that use them are sometimes in danger of spending much of this month's meeting arguing over the accuracy of the narrative about last month's meeting. Usually the disputed words do not matter. In fact most of the narration does not matter, as only the formal actions of the board as a whole are officially board business. Of course, a board member may wish to make a statement for the record and should not be prevented from doing so, but this is not the major purpose of minutes.

We recommend that you use your minutes to

1. Record the meeting's date, time, and attendance, and secretary's signature.
2. Record official actions of the board. Other than actions such as approving minutes of the previous meeting, these actions in Policy Governance will be the making or amending of policies.
3. Record affirming receipt of monitoring data, rendering appropriate responses to that data, collecting information and consideration of options for decisions, educational and ownership input, and other events that demonstrate diligence.
4. Upon request by individual board members, record statements for the record.

This use of minutes will ensure that they are brief and to the point. If there are errors, they will be easy to find, since there will be so much less extraneous material for you to wade through. It will also be easy to discern if the board is spending its time engaged in nongoverning busy-ness. Meetings that yield nothing for the minutes will quickly be noticed, and this will be an invaluable aid to maintaining the rigor that Policy Governance imposes on your board.

The Policy Manual

Your board policy manual should be where everything that the board has said, in its most recent form, can be found. It is therefore important that it be kept up-to-date and that every board member, as well as the CEO, has a copy.

After the implementation of Policy Governance and completion of Ends policies, virtually any decision a board makes is a decision that further defines or amends a policy that is already in existence. Recording these decisions in their appropriate places in the policy manual has two beneficial effects. First, it keeps the board focused on its policies so that they stay alive and familiar to board members. Second, it prevents the accumulation over time of board decisions growing scattered and untraceable. It would also prevent a massive build-up of policy material if it were not that Policy Governance boards make relatively few, but very important, decisions.

So even though a Policy Governance board makes fewer and weightier decisions than a traditional board, the manual is still subject to ongoing change. We suggest therefore that the manual be kept in a loose-leaf format. Ensure that policy decisions made by the board at its meetings get transferred to the manual by some timely and accurate mechanism. It is quite acceptable to expect the CEO to be responsible for this transfer taking place. If you choose the CEO to assure the ongoing policy manual accuracy, express this expectation in policy EL #2h, Communication and Support to the Board. Conversely, your board could decide that maintenance of the policy manual is a responsibility of the board secretary. If it does, it should make a Governance Process policy dealing with the secretary in order to explicitly state this expectation, since it exceeds the bylaws requirement that the secretary ensure the accuracy of documents.

Before further commentary about the policy manual, however, let's take a last look at the graphic presentation we have used thus far as an instructional tool. We can depict the policies demonstrated in Chapters Three through Seven by returning to that circle diagram. If your board had chosen to duplicate our pattern of policies, the resulting total of board policies would look like Figure 8.1.

It would be a good idea for your board to collect all the policy work covered in previous chapters, compiling those policies into a manual by category (Executive Limitations, Governance Process, Board-CEO Linkage, and Ends). Organize the policies by topic within the categories (shown in Resource A), not by level, as we

Figure 8.1. Board Policies Completed in All Four Categories.

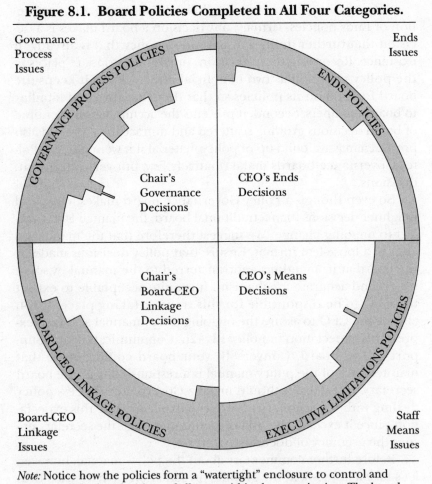

Note: Notice how the policies form a "watertight" enclosure to control and embrace all further decisions of all types within the organization. The board retains the right to change either the content or the depth of these policies at any time.

did in the policy development exercises. As an example, take all of the Treatment of Consumers policies (EL #2a plus EL #3a) in Executive Limitations and arrange them on a single page so that all that the board has said at various levels on that topic area is shown together. This will enable you to be sure about the amount of detail you included in each topic area with a minimum of searching.

Try to design a format for your policies that will accord them the status and the clarity they deserve as your governing pronouncements. These are the most important board documents and should look official rather than just like any number of other papers churned out by an organization. Make sure that it is apparent which policy category is being shown and what the policy topic is. Make sure that there is room for your secretary to attest to the accuracy of the content. There are many formats that will suffice, and we offer one in Figure 8.2 by way of example.

We have seen a number of creative approaches to organizing and customizing policy manuals. In one approach we liked, the board had each policy category produced on different-colored paper. Another useful technique a board used employed a small inset on each policy page, a graphic showing where on the circle diagram the particular policy showed up. Choose the method that suits you best. We are more concerned *that* you get the best possible use from your manual than *how* you do so.

Figure 8.2. Header Section of a Board Policy Form.

Policy of the Board	
Title:	Category:
Policy Serial No. _____ Date of Adoption: _____	Board secretary's affirmation of official board action adopting this policy. _____ Secretary

Note: The header section of a board policy form should look very official.

Making your work attractive and clear is important, since you will find that a well laid out and continually updated manual will be a useful tool in the maintenance of your governance system. We believe that board policies, as the only visible evidence of the voice of governance, should look the part.

A further benefit of ensuring a complete and up-to-date policy manual is its utility in the orientation of new board members. It is much more important to orient new board members to their own job rather than to staff jobs. Happily, the job of the board and the obligations of board members are clearly stated in policies found in the manual. What a contrast with traditional methods! Too often, new directors are unsure of the methods used by the board to govern. They find it hard to get an overview of the board's values and of what the board has said or not said. New members of your board, by contrast, will find that they can be familiar with the board's governance system and its current policies rapidly. Your vigilance about the board's manual not only will help today's board members maximize their contributions but will also ensure that new members speedily become contributors also.

Having set up the four sections in your manual for your policies, you might consider using the same loose-leaf notebook to add a further section into which monitoring reports can be placed when they are submitted to you. This will enable you to keep track of monitoring data over several months and will make it easier for you to be aware of developing trends in CEO performance.

Similarly, you may wish to keep bylaws and minutes in two additional sections of the notebook. Our advice earlier in this chapter about keeping your bylaws and minutes short could well stand you in good stead if you decide to do this! The advantage of keeping bylaws, monitoring reports, and minutes in the same binder as policies is that all the board's documents are in one handy place. Consider adding the Articles, Letters Patent, or founding legislation in the same way. Just be sure that the additions do not so burden the notebook that it falls out of regular use.

Next Chapter

In Chapter Nine, we describe the process of implementation, some safeguards and tips that might make the process more successful, and some ways to maintain the system. Except for the discussion of Ends in Chapter Seven, everything thus far has been preparing the governance vehicle to operate well. Now your challenge is to keep the governance system able to fulfill its mission "to see to it on behalf of the ownership that the organization achieves what it should and avoids unacceptable situations and conduct." Having gotten to this point is admirable, but the real work of governance has only just begun!

Chapter Nine

Implementation and Beyond

In this final chapter, we discuss some of the steps that we recommend using to support the full implementation of the Policy Governance model in your organization. Then we offer some advice regarding the ways in which your board can ensure that you do not jeopardize your initial investment of effort and time—ways to prevent the new system from deteriorating.

Implementation

If your board has been working through this book, preparing its policies according to the principles of the model, it will have a very complete set of means policies and a very incomplete set of Ends policies. Your board is virtually ready to implement the model at this point. Some steps are needed first, but contrary to what many of our clients guess, you do not need to complete all your Ends policies. As we noted in an earlier chapter, deciding Ends policies is the most time-consuming and highest-leverage work that your board will undertake. Fortunately, you do not have to wait until you have completed your Ends policies to begin governing in the new way. Indeed if you did wait, you would be in the absurd position of having spent time to prepare a large number of policies, and then not using them! For there is a sense in which we could say that Ends policies *are never finished.*

Here are the steps that we suggest:

1. *Adopt a global or tentative holding policy in Ends.* In the Ends category of policies, your board should have either a single, Level One Ends policy or a temporary policy whose purpose is to ensure that no major Ends changes will be made by the CEO while the

board does further Ends work. The tentative Ends policy we have used to temporarily plug the gap is worded like this: *Whatever Ends the board has stated or implied in previous decisions or approvals will stay unchanged, pending formal adoption of Ends policies.*

2. *Assess previous policies and decisions for inclusion.* After you have developed Executive Limitations, Governance Process, and Board-CEO Linkage policies, you should make sure that matters your board wanted to control in the past are adequately controlled in the new system. Do this by checking or having your CEO check previously adopted board documents. Be careful while doing this. You will almost certainly find that documents in an old format controlled CEO decisions at an unnecessary level of detail. Consequently, you cannot import them wholesale into your new policies and remain consistent with Policy Governance. Your new Executive Limitations policies have limited the CEO's choices to the point that you can accept any reasonable interpretation, so there should be little if anything in your old documents that you wish to add to the new ones. Do not allow this to be the opportunity for the dissenter on the board to undo your policy development work! The most common previous policies that our clients have wanted to preserve in some form have been those dealing with investments and conflict of interest. It is rare that they can be brought over into Policy Governance as previously written, but their broader aspects can be assimilated into the applicable new policies.

3. *Conduct a legal check.* For some boards, it may be wise to have your attorney do a legal check to make sure that the implementation of Policy Governance is not breaking any laws. Make sure that your attorney understands Policy Governance in general and the new use of the consent agenda in particular. We have never encountered organizations that have failed such a legal check, but doing one is prudent nonetheless. Conversely, our clients almost always find that their new policies have violated some aspects of their bylaws. If you find that this is the case, change your bylaws.

4. *Make a starter set of agendas.* Have some agendas ready for your meetings after implementation. You will already have broadly outlined your agenda plans in the applicable Governance Process policy. This should give all board members an indication of how the meeting time will be spent. If you are anxious about the meeting format, however, it may be useful to further define these initial meetings. You might be worried, for example, about how to have

a board meeting where there is no staff material on the agenda. Planning will eliminate this worry and boost confidence.

5. *Prepare your stakeholders.* Make sure that the people who watch your board know what it is doing. Some boards are more scrutinized than others. City councils and school boards are closely watched by the press, interest groups, unions, and a number of other interested parties. Boards that are less public may be less scrutinized, but they should still be aware that their new governance style may appear odd or even irresponsible to staff, unions, members, and other uninformed groups. So invest in some PR! Let your publics know that you are planning to govern in a manner that will make you meaningfully accountable for the organization on behalf of those who own it. So radical a change as a new governance model is best shouted from the rooftops rather than slipped in while no one is watching. Shout it out!

6. *Move in one fell swoop.* Set a date on which the model comes into effect, and pass a motion stating that as of that date, all previous board policies and other decisions are set aside, and your new policies are in effect. You may feel that this is a sudden and perhaps precipitous way to proceed. We would answer that implementing Policy Governance involves a change of such magnitude that it can be likened to jumping from one trapeze to another. It is important to take as much time as is necessary in setting up the second trapeze, testing it, and getting ready to jump. But jumping has to happen quickly and once. Incremental change within a paradigm can be done in phases; phasing in a shift from one paradigm to another can be like trying to change from playing baseball to playing football gradually!

7. *Gain confidence through data.* Expect to receive monitoring data on the schedule you have already determined just as soon as implementation begins. Be forewarned that the system may not work as well right away as it will later. After all, the staff have a lot of changes to make in their data gathering and analysis.

Maintaining the System

When your board starts to use Policy Governance, that is, when it implements the policies it has worked so hard on, your board life will change beyond recognition. You will find that you will have the chance to talk about and decide issues of great importance. You will be in control of an organization without maintaining the fiction that after-the-fact decision making is really leading. You will be, if we may use a nautical analogy, on the bridge looking at the horizon rather than in the engine room checking oil levels. For most board members, this is a change that is welcomed and enjoyed.

But there are challenges too. The way in which you and your board have reacted to situations and input will have to change in order to maintain the governance you have chosen. Turnover of board members, organizational crises, and consumer complaints will challenge your resolve to remain consistent. In short, a high level of board discipline is required by Policy Governance. Your board and every board will find numerous reasons to be undisciplined and to act in a manner inconsistent with your resolve. The cost of such lack of discipline is high. First, the ownership of the organization is cheated by a board that fails to perform the job of governance. Second, your CEO and staff will learn that your board will remain unpredictable, capricious, and untrustworthy. When staff members perceive a board as untrustworthy, they will spend time and resources neutralizing the risk to them of its unpredictability. Third, your ability to recruit and retain board members who wish to make a difference will be impaired if the board acts erratically.

Here are some techniques, mentioned during this book, that we reiterate in discussing your challenge to maintain your governance system.

1. *Board member recruitment.* If your board has control over its recruitment, it should be sure to let candidates know before they come onto the board that the system used is Policy Governance. Let your prospective new members know how your board sees the job of governance. They can then make an informed choice about their willingness to serve. If your board does not control but can influence the selection of board members, it should tell those who do make the selections the characteristics required in new members.

2. *Board member orientation.* Do this before the new board member's first meeting if at all possible. Orient the member to the board job, since this is the one he or she needs to know about. Explaining staff jobs will be interesting but incidental information. Use your board policy manual as a resource. It contains all the

current governing values and will help your new colleague to quickly understand what the board has said about its role and its expectations of the organization. Some boards use buddy systems, pairing a new board member with an experienced one. This can be very helpful, as it compels the experienced board member to be as knowledgeable as possible in order to accurately teach the new one.

3. *Board self-evaluation.* Your board decided some aspects of self-evaluation when it developed its Governance Process policies. We have already noted that we recommend frequent self-evaluation and prefer to see boards self-evaluate at each meeting. We do not mean to imply that boards should allow such evaluation to take a major amount of time. It can be accomplished rather speedily. Remember that monitoring is always against criteria and that the policies are your criteria. Hence board self-evaluation is the comparison of how the board conducted itself to how it said it would conduct itself. Take a different one of your Governance Process policies at each meeting, and have someone critique the board according to the criteria in the policy.

4. *Education.* Your board should have access to materials or conferences that will support and enhance its understanding of governance. Note that most available board literature is not written from a Policy Governance perspective but from a traditional perspective. Take great care in learning from these materials. They do contain a great deal of wisdom that can be helpful, but you have to read them with your Policy Governance screen well in place. There is little reason to learn from someone's wisdom about personnel committees, for example, when you know boards should never have one. On the other hand, there may be much to learn about recruiting techniques, as long as you remember to use board member qualifications that are consistent with the Policy Governance job to be done. For example, do not recruit people because they are accountants and lawyers; recruit them for their ability to express appropriate board leadership. Also be a discerning reader of materials that claim to be about Policy Governance; be sure they were prepared by someone who knows the model!

When the Going Gets Tough, the Tough Go Back to Basics

Not uncommonly, a board that is using Policy Governance confidently may find that it is sorely tempted to revert to more traditional methods when a crisis or apparent crisis arises. Ostensibly, a board uses Policy Governance because it is convinced that it enables governing responsibly and diligently. That being the case, to *not use it* during a crisis flies in the face of reason, equivalent to a pilot who forsakes the instruments just when they are needed the most.

Nonetheless, there will be events that test you and can entice you back toward more familiar ground. We've seen boards making great headway in governance improvement that absolutely lost it when some problem or threat arose, the CEO failed, or some other unfortunate event occurred. They failed to understand that when things get rough is precisely when you need the best model you can get. Here are some examples.

1. *Your policies are realistic, and your monitoring report shows an out-of-compliance financial situation.* If your board wants to discuss how the problem should be fixed or wants to fix it itself, it will never know if it has a CEO who can handle this and other situations. The appropriate response to this problem is to agree with the CEO on a realistic time frame for the CEO to fix the problem and keep it fixed. Of course, if the financial situation is sufficiently dire, the board's best judgment may be to replace the CEO forthwith.

2. *Your funding is cut.* If your board has addressed the cost component of Ends policies in percentage terms, it may not need to do anything about this situation. If it used dollar amounts in its Ends policies, it may need to restate them. Your board should *not* be involved in decisions about which programs or staff to cut. These are means issues, and you have told the CEO that he or she can make these decisions within the constraints of your Executive Limitations policies.

3. *A board member or even the whole board has been approached by a consumer who has a complaint.* It will be tempting to try to solve the "problem," but remember that a complaint is an allegation and there may not be a problem. There will always be dissatisfied consumers. The board in its Treatment of Consumers policy has spelled out what forms of treatment it will not tolerate. The board should inform the CEO and then go through the following decision process. First, the board should ask itself whether any of its policies would have been violated if the allegation were true. Second, if no policies would have been violated, there is nothing for the board to do unless it feels existing policy is inadequate. If so,

then the board considers expanding its policy. Third, if a policy may have been violated, the board should acquire information that would monitor the policy in question, sticking with its rules for monitoring already established in its Monitoring CEO Performance policy. The board has the freedom, of course, to decide that the situation does not warrant such an extra monitoring but that it can wait for the regular monitoring as scheduled. Fourth, when monitoring occurs, the board should respond to the data by assessing whether or not the organization is in compliance with a reasonable interpretation of its policy.

4. *The board is worried about its responsibility to raise funds.* The board's primary responsibility is to govern. It may or may not have a responsibility to raise funds. The need to raise funds comes about when the board demands Ends that cannot be attained without fund raising. Fund raising, therefore, while obviously a means issue, is Ends-driven. The board may decide to add the acquisition of funds to its own job list, its values-added, as listed in its Board Job Description policy. If it does not choose to do so, the CEO is left with total accountability for producing whatever is needed to attain the Ends, including the necessary funds. Of course, the board can limit some of the CEO's fund-raising options by enacting an Executive Limitations policy. If a board decides that it will take on only a part of the responsibility for acquiring funds, such as producing names of prospective donors, it will add that aspect to its job list. (The board then holds itself and not the CEO accountable for that part of the job.) The effect of this action is that all other aspects of fund raising are therefore part of the CEO's job. Knowing exactly which parts of the total fund-raising job the board officially commits itself to will prevent the familiar scenario of the fund-raising staff and board members becoming confused and frustrated about respective roles.

Policy Governance as a system of decision making and leadership is designed, like a good knife, to get better with use. You will have no problem with the model deteriorating if you follow all the principles we have outlined. You will have deterioration, and that very soon, if you fudge on the principles or fail to follow the necessary board discipline.

For example, if something occurs on-staff that upsets a majority of board members, yet that something is not a violation of board policy, what should the board do? If in doubt, re-read the previous section about the board response to a consumer complaint. The same principle applies. Such an occasion should be seen as an opportunity not to set the "something" right but to adjust the system if necessary to make it even stronger. The board does not accost its CEO, nor does the board move into staff means to fix the problem or even direct how it will be fixed. The board admits that its own policy is insufficient, if this is the case, then debates how to change it. The CEO has been fairly treated, the CEO trusts that the board will keep its word, the board policy is better than before, and the board's confidence is stronger.

In the end, maintaining Policy Governance is a serious board responsibility. It is not the staff's. And due to the design of the model, *maintaining* Policy Governance simply means *using* it consistently and boldly.

Now that you have come this far with us, we are going to have to disappoint you. Policy Governance itself is not an Ends issue. No organization exists in order to use Policy Governance. It is a means—a board means, to be sure, not a staff means, but a means nonetheless. As such, it is a tool provided for the better expression of board leadership—an advanced kind of leadership capable of leading leaders.

That means that with Policy Governance in place, your board work is not over. It is merely beginning. For having the best tools in the world builds no bridges and crosses no oceans. Now the real work begins.

We can predict that from now on your workload as a board will be almost entirely in three areas:

1. *Education.* You may spend more than half your time learning, not about staff jobs but about issues that will enable you to make informed, visionary, creative decisions largely about Ends. This learning will come from various sources that you will select. Some will be from the ownership—those who morally own your organization, those whom you represent as board members. It will take carefully developed strategies to get to these people and to be sure you are getting a fair representation of their views rather than the views only of the louder constituents. Remember not to confuse owner input with the input of disgruntled customers. Some of

the learning will come from invited experts or other outsiders who have special knowledge or experience. How long has it been since you had a futurist address the particular interest of your organization? Some of the learning will come from your CEO and staff. They are a rich source of ideas and passion.

2. *Ends debate.* The previous focus is almost entirely intended to prepare you for the Ends struggle. Entertain diverse points of view, see that they are argued vehemently, study the long-term effects of various Ends choices. Most of your board year should be involved in addressing various portions of the Ends question. Do not confine this work to an annual retreat, even though a retreat setting can well serve as a component of your year-long sequence of Ends re-examination. This is the heart of board work, so do not fear to be absolutely and unapologetically obsessive about it. A board meeting that does not deal with at least one substantive Ends issue is a board meeting that didn't quite make it.

3. *Keeping the faith.* Board discipline will require conscious attention. Don't expect discipline to be something you have rather than something you continually pursue. That is, discipline is an explicit issue for board discussion at every meeting. When we suggested that you do self-evaluation no less than once per meeting, this is part of what we meant. But go beyond self-evaluation; discuss how you can get better, how you can stray less, how you can waste less time. Boards we have known have tried naming and, we hope, rotating board members as "governance cops" in a humorous but effective way to spotlight sticking to the rules. This may sound awkward, but we suppose a pilot's going through an explicit checklist on *every* flight feels just as awkward.

So we leave you with your challenge. We salute your commitment, your effort, and your dreams. We hope you have fun and grow as people while answering responsibly to your considerable accountability. Never forget that your job is not so much to review last month, keep up with your staff's unending supply of activities, or be managers at arm's length. Your job is to lead, to be spokespersons for meaningful values, to model bigness of spirit, to be a powerful representative of your ownership (and sometimes its gadfly conscience!), and ultimately to see that tomorrow is created in a better image.

We live in this world, too. We are in your debt.

Resources

A Sample Board Policy Manual

In Resource A, we present a group of policies that might well comprise all those needed in the means policies—the categories we call Executive Limitations, Board-CEO Linkage, and Governance Process. Certainly a given board might have need of more than these, but there is no way to illustrate all the possible policies a board might choose to have. The possibilities are endless. We are fortunate, however, that the nature of means policies enables us to illustrate a number of fairly common, relatively complete policy samples. Boards are surprisingly similar in what they choose to say in these areas.

In the case of board means, the similarity is inevitable because they are so guided by the principles of the model. Conversely, staff means are guided by the board's values of prudence and ethics, also a phenomenon quite alike from one board to another. Ends will be different, so we have elected to display them differently. These will be shown in Resource B.

We chose in Chapters Four through Seven to take you with us through policy making by looking at one level after another—first, second, third, and a few times, fourth. We used this level-by-level approach across all topics. In assembling a policy manual for everyday use, however, you will find it far more helpful to have your policies grouped by topic. Such an arrangement shows the various levels within that topic all together. This is the format we will employ in the coming pages.

Please keep in mind that we are not proposing that the specific wording of these samples is necessarily correct for your board.

Indeed, if you circumvent the admittedly painstaking process of developing your own policies, even though they may turn out to be much like ours, you will miss the main point here. Whatever the language used, these must be *your* policies. We can guarantee that the policies displayed are (1) model-consistent, (2) very like those actually developed by our clients with our guidance, and (3) a quite workable starter set.

Here is a registry of the policies shown:

EXECUTIVE LIMITATIONS	Global Executive Constraint
	Treatment of Consumers
	Treatment of Staff
	Financial Planning and Budgeting
	Financial Condition and Activities
	Emergency CEO Succession
	Asset Protection
	Compensation and Benefits
	Communication and Support to the Board
	Ends Focus of Grants or Contracts
GOVERNANCE PROCESS	Global Governance Commitment
	Governing Style
	Board Job Description
	Agenda Planning
	Chairperson's Role
	Board Members' Code of Conduct
	Board Committee Principles
	Cost of Governance
BOARD-CEO LINKAGE	Global Board-CEO Linkage
	Unity of Control
	Accountability of the CEO
	Delegation to the CEO
	Monitoring CEO Performance

POLICY TYPE: EXECUTIVE LIMITATIONS

POLICY TITLE: GLOBAL EXECUTIVE CONSTRAINT

The CEO shall not cause or allow any practice, activity, decision, or orga-
nizational circumstance that is either unlawful, imprudent, or in violation
of commonly accepted business and professional ethics.

POLICY TYPE: EXECUTIVE LIMITATIONS

POLICY TITLE: TREATMENT OF CONSUMERS

With respect to interactions with consumers or those applying to be con-
sumers, the CEO shall not cause or allow conditions, procedures, or deci-
sions that are unsafe, undignified, unnecessarily intrusive, or that fail to
provide appropriate confidentiality or privacy.

Accordingly, he or she shall not:

1. Use application forms that elicit information for which there is no clear necessity.
2. Use methods of collecting, reviewing, transmitting, or storing client information that fail to protect against improper access to the material elicited.
3. Maintain facilities that fail to provide a reasonable level of privacy, both visual and aural.
4. Fail to establish with consumers a clear understanding of what may be expected and what may not be expected from the service offered.
5. Fail to inform consumers of this policy, or to provide a grievance process to those who believe they have not been accorded a reasonable interpretation of their rights under this policy.

POLICY TYPE: EXECUTIVE LIMITATIONS

POLICY TITLE: TREATMENT OF STAFF

With respect to the treatment of paid and volunteer staff, the CEO may not cause or allow conditions that are unfair or undignified.
Accordingly, he or she shall not:

1. Operate without written personnel policies that clarify personnel rules for staff, provide for effective handling of grievances, and protect against wrongful conditions such as nepotism and grossly preferential treatment for personal reasons.
2. Discriminate against any staff member for expressing an ethical dissent.
3. Prevent staff from grieving to the board when (1) internal grievance procedures have been exhausted and (2) the employee alleges either that (a) board policy has been violated to his or her detriment or (b) board policy does not adequately protect his or her human rights.
4. Fail to acquaint staff with their rights under this policy.

POLICY TYPE: EXECUTIVE LIMITATIONS

POLICY TITLE: FINANCIAL PLANNING AND BUDGETING

Financial planning for any fiscal year or the remaining part of any fiscal year shall not deviate materially from the board's Ends priorities, risk fiscal jeopardy, or fail to be derived from a multiyear plan.
Accordingly, the CEO shall not allow budgeting that:

1. Contains too little information to enable credible projection of revenues and expenses, separation of capital and operational items, cash flow, and disclosure of planning assumptions.
2. Plans the expenditure in any fiscal year of more funds than are conservatively projected to be received in that period.
3. Reduces the current assets at any time to less than twice current liabilities [or allows cash to drop below a safety reserve of less than $_____ at any time].
4. Provides less for board prerogatives during the year than is set forth in the Cost of Governance policy.

POLICY TYPE: EXECUTIVE LIMITATIONS

POLICY TITLE: FINANCIAL CONDITION AND ACTIVITIES

With respect to the actual, ongoing financial condition and activities, the CEO shall not cause or allow the development of fiscal jeopardy or a material deviation of actual expenditures from board priorities established in Ends policies.

Accordingly, the CEO shall not:

1. Expend more funds than have been received in the fiscal year to date, unless the debt guideline (to follow) is met.
2. Indebt the organization in an amount greater than can be repaid by certain, otherwise unencumbered revenues within sixty days.
3. Use any long-term reserves.
4. Conduct interfund shifting in amounts greater than can be restored to a condition of discrete fund balances by certain, otherwise unencumbered revenue within thirty days.
5. Fail to settle payroll and debts in a timely manner.
6. Allow tax payments or other government-ordered payments or filings to be overdue or inaccurately filed.
7. Make a single purchase or commitment of greater than $_____.
8. Acquire, encumber, or dispose of real property.
9. Fail to aggressively pursue receivables after a reasonable grace period.

POLICY TYPE: EXECUTIVE LIMITATIONS

POLICY TITLE: EMERGENCY CEO SUCCESSION

In order to protect the board from sudden loss of CEO services, the CEO may have no fewer than two other executives familiar with board and CEO issues and processes.

POLICY TYPE: EXECUTIVE LIMITATIONS

POLICY TITLE: ASSET PROTECTION

The CEO shall not allow the assets to be unprotected, inadequately maintained, or unnecessarily risked.

Accordingly, he or she may not:

1. Fail to insure against theft and casualty losses to at least 80 percent of replacement value and against liability losses to board members, staff, and the organization itself in an amount greater than the average for comparable organizations.
2. Allow unbonded personnel access to material amounts of funds.
3. Subject plant and equipment to improper wear and tear or insufficient maintenance.
4. Unnecessarily expose the organization, its board, or staff to claims of liability.
5. Make any purchase (1) wherein normally prudent protection has not been given against conflict of interest; (2) of over $_____ without having obtained comparative prices and quality; (3) of over $_____ without a stringent method of assuring the balance of long-term quality and cost.
6. Fail to protect intellectual property, information, and files from loss or significant damage.
7. Receive, process, or disburse funds under controls that are insufficient to meet the board-appointed auditor's standards.
8. Invest or hold operating capital in insecure instruments, including uninsured checking accounts and bonds of less than AA rating, or in non-interest-bearing accounts except where necessary to facilitate ease in operational transactions.
9. Endanger the organization's public image or credibility, particularly in ways that would hinder its accomplishment of mission.

POLICY TYPE: EXECUTIVE LIMITATIONS

POLICY TITLE: COMPENSATION AND BENEFITS

With respect to employment, compensation, and benefits to employees, consultants, contract workers, and volunteers, the CEO shall not cause or allow jeopardy to fiscal integrity or public image.

Accordingly, he or she may not:

1. Change his or her own compensation and benefits.
2. Promise or imply permanent or guaranteed employment.
3. Establish current compensation and benefits that deviate materially from the geographic or professional market for the skills employed.
4. Create compensation obligations over a longer term than revenues can be safely projected, in no event longer than one year, and in all events subject to losses in revenue.
5. Establish or change pension benefits so as to cause unpredictable or inequitable situations, including those that
   a. Incur unfunded liabilities.
   b. Provide less than some basic level of benefits to all full-time employees, though differential benefits to encourage longevity are not prohibited.
   c. Allow any employee to lose benefits already accrued from any foregoing plan.
   d. Treat the CEO differently from other key employees.

POLICY TYPE: EXECUTIVE LIMITATIONS

POLICY TITLE: COMMUNICATION AND SUPPORT
                 TO THE BOARD

The CEO shall not permit the board to be uninformed or unsupported in its work.

Accordingly, he or she shall not:

1. Neglect to submit monitoring data required by the board (see policy on Monitoring CEO Performance) in a timely, accurate, and understandable fashion, directly addressing provisions of board policies being monitored.
2. Let the board be unaware of relevant trends, anticipated adverse media coverage, material external and internal changes, particularly changes in the assumptions upon which any board policy has previously been established.
3. Fail to advise the board if, in the CEO's opinion, the board is not in compliance with its own policies on Governance Process and Board-CEO Linkage, particularly in the case of board behavior that is detrimental to the work relationship between the board and the CEO.
4. Fail to marshal for the board as many staff and external points of view, issues, and options as needed for fully informed board choices.
5. Present information in unnecessarily complex or lengthy form or in a form that fails to differentiate among information of three types: monitoring, decision preparation, and other.
6. Fail to provide a mechanism for official board, officer, or committee communications.
7. Fail to deal with the board as a whole except when (a) fulfilling individual requests for information or (b) responding to officers or committees duly charged by the board.
8. Fail to report in a timely manner an actual or anticipated noncompliance with any policy of the board.
9. Fail to supply for the consent agenda all items delegated to the CEO yet required by law or contract to be board-approved, along with the monitoring assurance pertaining thereto.

POLICY TYPE: EXECUTIVE LIMITATIONS

POLICY TITLE: ENDS FOCUS OF GRANTS OR
CONTRACTS

The CEO may not enter into any grant or contract arrangements that fail to emphasize primarily the production of Ends and, secondarily, the avoidance of unacceptable means.

Accordingly, the CEO shall not:

1. Fail to prohibit particular methods and activities to preclude grant funds from being used in imprudent, unlawful, or unethical ways.
2. Fail to assess and consider an applicant's capability to produce appropriately targeted, efficient results.
3. Fund specific methods except when doing so for research purposes, when the result to be achieved is knowledge about differential effectiveness of various methods.

POLICY TYPE: GOVERNANCE PROCESS

POLICY TITLE: GLOBAL GOVERNANCE COMMITMENT

The purpose of the board, on behalf of [identify the ownership here], is to see to it that [name of organization] (1) achieves appropriate results for appropriate persons at an appropriate cost and (2) avoids unacceptable actions and situations.

POLICY TYPE: GOVERNANCE PROCESS

POLICY TITLE: GOVERNING STYLE

The board will govern with an emphasis on (1) outward vision rather than internal preoccupation, (2) encouragement of diversity in viewpoints, (3) strategic leadership more than administrative detail, (4) clear distinction of board and chief executive roles, (5) collective rather than individual decisions, (6) future rather than past or present, and (7) proactivity rather than reactivity.

Accordingly,

1. The board will cultivate a sense of group responsibility. The board, not the staff, will be responsible for excellence in governing. The board will be the initiator of policy, not merely a reactor to staff initiatives. The board will use the expertise of individual members to enhance the ability of the board as a body rather than to substitute individual judgments for the board's values. The board will allow no officer, individual, or committee of the board to hinder or be an excuse for not fulfilling board commitments.

2. The board will direct, control, and inspire the organization through the careful establishment of broad written policies reflecting the board's values and perspectives about ends to be achieved and means to be avoided. The board's major policy focus will be on the intended long-term effects outside the organization, not on the administrative or programmatic means of attaining those effects.

3. The board will enforce upon itself whatever discipline is needed to govern with excellence. Discipline will apply to matters such as attendance, preparation, policy-making principles, respect of roles, and ensuring continuance of governance capability. Continual board development will include orientation of new board members in the board's governance process and periodic board discussion of process improvement.

4. The board will monitor and discuss the board's process and performance at each meeting. Self-monitoring will include comparison of board activity and discipline to policies in the Governance Process and Board-CEO Linkage categories.

POLICY TYPE: GOVERNANCE PROCESS

POLICY TITLE: BOARD JOB DESCRIPTION

The job of the board is to represent the [identify the ownership here] in determining and demanding appropriate organizational performance.
Accordingly,

1. The board will produce the link between the organization and the ownership.
2. The board will produce written governing policies that, at the broadest levels, address each category of organizational decision.
    a. *Ends:* Organizational products, effects, benefits, outcomes, recipients, and their relative worth (what good for which recipients at what cost).
    b. *Executive Limitations:* Constraints on executive authority that establish the prudence and ethics boundaries within which all executive activity and decisions must take place.
    c. *Governance Process:* Specification of how the board conceives, carries out, and monitors its own task.
    d. *Board-CEO Linkage:* How power is delegated and its proper use monitored; the CEO role, authority, and accountability.
3. The board will produce assurance of CEO performance (against policies in 2a and 2b).

POLICY TYPE: GOVERNANCE PROCESS

POLICY TITLE: AGENDA PLANNING

To accomplish its job products with a governance style consistent with board policies, the board will follow an annual agenda that (1) completes re-exploration of Ends policies annually and (2) continually improves board performance through board education and enriched input and deliberation.
  Accordingly,

1. The cycle will conclude each year on the last day of September so that administrative planning and budgeting can be based on accomplishing a one-year segment of the board's most recent statement of long-term Ends.
2. The cycle will start with the board's development of its agenda for the next year.
    a. Consultations with selected groups in the ownership or other methods of gaining ownership input will be determined and arranged in the first quarter, to be held during the balance of the year.
    b. Governance education and education related to Ends determination (for example, presentations by futurists, demographers, advocacy groups, and staff) will be arranged in the first quarter, to be held during the balance of the year.
3. Throughout the year, the board will attend to consent agenda items as expeditiously as possible.
4. CEO monitoring will be included on the agenda if monitoring reports show policy violations or if policy criteria are to be debated.
5. CEO remuneration will be decided after a review of monitoring reports received in the last year during the month of February.

POLICY TYPE: GOVERNANCE PROCESS

POLICY TITLE: CHAIRPERSON'S ROLE

The chairperson assures the integrity of the board's process and, secondarily, occasionally represents the board to outside parties.
    Accordingly,

1. The job result of the chairperson is that the board behaves consistently with its own rules and those legitimately imposed upon it from outside the organization.
   a. Meeting discussion content will be only those issues which, according to board policy, clearly belong to the board to decide, not the CEO.
   b. Deliberation will be fair, open, and thorough but also timely, orderly, and kept to the point.
2. The authority of the chairperson consists in making decisions that fall within topics covered by board policies on Governance Process and Board-CEO Linkage, except where the board specifically delegates portions of this authority to others. The chairperson is authorized to use any reasonable interpretation of the provisions in these policies.
   a. The chairperson is empowered to chair board meetings, with all the commonly accepted power of that position (for example, ruling, recognizing).
   b. The chairperson has no authority to make decisions about policies created by the board within Ends and Executive Limitations policy areas. Therefore, the chairperson has no authority to supervise or direct the CEO.
   c. The chairperson may represent the board to outside parties in announcing board-stated positions and in stating chair decisions and interpretations within the area delegated to her or him.
   d. The chairperson may delegate this authority but remains accountable for its use.

POLICY TYPE: GOVERNANCE PROCESS

POLICY TITLE: BOARD MEMBERS' CODE OF CONDUCT

The board commits itself and its members to ethical, businesslike, and lawful conduct, including proper use of authority and appropriate decorum when acting as board members.

Accordingly,

1. Members must represent unconflicted loyalty to the interests of the ownership. This accountability supersedes any conflicting loyalty such as that to advocacy or interest groups and membership on other boards or staffs. It also supersedes the personal interest of any board member acting as a consumer of the organization's services.

2. Members must avoid conflict of interest with respect to their fiduciary responsibility.

   a. There must be no self-dealing or any conduct of private business or personal services between any board member and the organization except as procedurally controlled to assure openness, competitive opportunity, and equal access to inside information.

   b. When the board is to decide upon an issue about which a member has an unavoidable conflict of interest, that member shall absent herself or himself without comment from not only the vote but also from the deliberation.

   c. Board members must not use their positions to obtain employment for themselves, family members, or close associates. Should a member desire employment, he or she must first resign.

   d. Members will annually disclose their involvements with other organizations, with vendors, or any other associations that might produce a conflict.

3. Board members may not attempt to exercise individual authority over the organization except as explicitly set forth in board policies.

   a. Members' interaction with the CEO or with staff must recognize the lack of authority vested in individuals except when explicitly board-authorized.

b. Members' interactions with public, press, or other entities must recognize the same limitation and the inability of any board member to speak for the board except to repeat explicitly stated board decisions.

c. Members will give no consequence or voice to individual judgments of CEO or staff performance.

4. Members will respect the confidentiality appropriate to issues of a sensitive nature.

POLICY TYPE: GOVERNANCE PROCESS

POLICY TITLE: BOARD COMMITTEE PRINCIPLES

Board committees, when used, will be assigned so as to reinforce the wholeness of the board's job and so as never to interfere with delegation from board to CEO.

Accordingly,

1. Board committees are to help the board do its job, never to help or advise the staff. Committees ordinarily will assist the board by preparing policy alternatives and implications for board deliberation. In keeping with the board's broader focus, board committees will normally not have dealings with current staff operations.

2. Board committees may not speak or act for the board except when formally given such authority for specific and time-limited purposes. Expectations and authority will be carefully stated in order not to conflict with authority delegated to the CEO.

3. Board committees cannot exercise authority over staff. Because the CEO works for the full board, he or she will not be required to obtain approval of a board committee before an executive action.

4. Board committees are to avoid over-identification with organizational parts rather than the whole. Therefore a board committee that has helped the board create policy on some topic will not be used to monitor organizational performance on that same topic.

5. Committees will be used sparingly and ordinarily in an ad hoc capacity.

6. This policy applies to any group that is formed by board action, whether or not it is called a committee and regardless whether the group includes board members. It does not apply to committees formed under the authority of the CEO.

POLICY TYPE: GOVERNANCE PROCESS

POLICY TITLE: COST OF GOVERNANCE

Because poor governance costs more than learning to govern well, the board will invest in its governance capacity.
Accordingly,

1. Board skills, methods, and supports will be sufficient to assure governing with excellence.
   a. Training and retraining will be used liberally to orient new members and candidates for membership, as well as to maintain and increase existing member skills and understandings.
   b. Outside monitoring assistance will be arranged so that the board can exercise confident control over organizational performance. This includes but is not limited to fiscal audit.
   c. Outreach mechanisms will be used as needed to ensure the board's ability to listen to owner viewpoints and values.
2. Costs will be prudently incurred, though not at the expense of endangering the development and maintenance of superior capability.
   a. Up to $_____ in fiscal year _____ for training, including attendance at conferences and workshops.
   b. Up to $_____ in fiscal year _____ for audit and other third-party monitoring of organizational performance.
   c. Up to $_____ in fiscal year _____ for surveys, focus groups, opinion analyses, and meeting costs.

POLICY TYPE: BOARD-CEO LINKAGE

POLICY TITLE: GLOBAL BOARD-CEO LINKAGE

The board's sole official connection to the operational organization, its achievements, and conduct will be through a Chief Executive Officer.

POLICY TYPE: BOARD-CEO LINKAGE

POLICY TITLE: UNITY OF CONTROL

Only decisions of the board acting as a body are binding on the CEO.
Accordingly,

1. Decisions or instructions of individual board members, officers, or committees are not binding on the CEO except in rare instances when the board has specifically authorized such exercise of authority.
2. In the case of board members or committees requesting information or assistance without board authorization, the CEO can refuse such requests that require, in the CEO's opinion, a material amount of staff time or funds, or are disruptive.

POLICY TYPE: BOARD-CEO LINKAGE

POLICY TITLE: ACCOUNTABILITY OF THE CEO

The CEO is the board's only link to operational achievement and conduct, so that all authority and accountability of staff, as far as the board is concerned, is considered the authority and accountability of the CEO.
Accordingly,

1. The board will never give instructions to persons who report directly or indirectly to the CEO.
2. The board will refrain from evaluating, either formally or informally, any staff other than the CEO.

3. The board will view CEO performance as identical to organizational performance, so that organizational accomplishment of board-stated Ends and avoidance of board-proscribed means will be viewed as successful CEO performance.

POLICY TYPE: BOARD-CEO LINKAGE

POLICY TITLE: DELEGATION TO THE CEO

The board will instruct the CEO through written policies that prescribe the organizational Ends to be achieved and describe organizational situations and actions to be avoided, allowing the CEO to use any reasonable interpretation of these policies.

Accordingly,

1. The board will develop policies instructing the CEO to achieve certain results, for certain recipients, at a specified cost. These policies will be developed systematically from the broadest, most general level to more defined levels, and will be called *Ends policies.*
2. The board will develop policies that limit the latitude the CEO may exercise in choosing the organizational means. These policies will be developed systematically from the broadest, most general level to more defined levels, and they will be called *Executive Limitations policies.*
3. As long as the CEO uses *any reasonable interpretation* of the board's Ends and Executive Limitations policies, the CEO is authorized to establish all further policies, make all decisions, take all actions, establish all practices, and develop all activities.
4. The board may change its Ends and Executive Limitations policies, thereby shifting the boundary between board and CEO domains. By doing so, the board changes the latitude of choice given to the CEO. But as long as any particular delegation is in place, the board will respect and support the CEO's choices.

POLICY TYPE: BOARD-CEO LINKAGE

POLICY TITLE: MONITORING CEO PERFORMANCE

Systematic and rigorous monitoring of CEO job performance will be solely against the only expected CEO job outputs: organizational accomplishment of board policies on Ends and organizational operation within the boundaries established in board policies on Executive Limitations.

Accordingly,

1. Monitoring is simply to determine the degree to which board policies are being met. Data that do not do this will not be considered to be monitoring data.
2. The board will acquire monitoring data by one or more of three methods: (a) by internal report, in which the CEO discloses compliance information to the board, (b) by external report, in which an external, disinterested third party selected by the board assesses compliance with board policies, and (c) by direct board inspection, in which a designated member or members of the board assess compliance with the appropriate policy criteria.
3. In every case, the standard for compliance shall be *any reasonable CEO interpretation* of the board policy being monitored.
4. All policies that instruct the CEO will be monitored at a frequency and by a method chosen by the board. The board can monitor any policy at any time by any method, but will ordinarily depend on a routine schedule.

Policy	Method	Frequency
Treatment of Consumers	Internal	Annually
Treatment of Staff	Internal	Annually
Financial Planning and Budgeting	Internal	Quarterly
Financial Condition and Activities	Internal	Quarterly
	External	Annually
Emergency CEO Succession	Internal	Annually
Compensation and Benefits	Internal	Annually
	External	Biannually
Communication and Support	Direct Inspection	Annually

[*Note:* As Ends policies are developed, they would be added to this list.]

Sample Ends Policies

In Resource A, we presented a sample policy manual composed of policies in three of the four categories of board policy. Those policy samples are consistent with each other, as they would be in an actual governance setting. We explained why those three categories of policies seem very similar across all organization types. But as we also explained, Ends are not like that. They differ widely from one organization to another. Consequently, in order to show some sample Ends policies, we will display policies that are not consistent with each other. They might be found in very different organizations. Obviously, by the nature of various purposes, the Ends of hospitals, city government, social service agencies, trade associations, and others will differ markedly.

Hence we separate sample Ends policies from the others and present them to you in this section, not as a group that would ever appear together but as they might be found in varying settings. In some cases we have used policies attributed to actual organizations. In those cases we make no representation that the organization currently uses the policy shown, only that it either drafted or adopted it at some point in the past. In some of the policies derived from real organizations, we have shortened the language for our own purposes of illustration.

Again, we do not present these policies as examples of how much detail a board should pursue or as examples of a content that we support. They are samples of format and model-consistent statements. For example, the policy dealing with cancer research goes into much greater detail than we would conceive a board ever going into. Keep in mind that the Ends policy shown for any given organization, real or hypothetical, would be only one of several Ends policies that would have been developed.

You will also notice that different organizations take different viewpoints with respect to the use of words like *purpose* and *mission.* Some keep their global Ends policy on a separate policy page from subparts of that global statement; some do not. These are cosmetic issues. The only relevant aspect is whether Policy Governance principles continue to be observed faithfully in the origination and construction of the policies. To conserve space, we have omitted illustration of date of adoption, policy serial number that a given board might adopt, and the board secretary's signature line for attesting to the formal board action that made the policy official.

POLICY TYPE:	ENDS
POLICY TITLE:	PURPOSE

The purpose of the American Association of Colleges of Podiatric Medicine *is a strong system of academic podiatric medicine.*

1. Information to member institutions required for system excellence.
   a. Information about academic podiatric medicine institutional characteristics.
   b. Information about the health care environment that poses significant threat or opportunity to academic podiatric medicine or is relevant to interdisciplinary communication.
2. Academic podiatric medicine is seen as essential, vital, and professionally competent.
3. Beneficial venues of synergistic interconnectedness among elements of the system.
4. Cost-saving economies of scale in institutional purchasing.

Note: Our thanks to the American Association of Colleges of Podiatric Medicine for the use of this policy. We have abridged their actual document.

POLICY TYPE: ENDS

POLICY TITLE: PURPOSE

The purpose of the Municipal Symphony Orchestra is that *our heritage of classical music will be relevant to all aspects of our personal and community lives.*

1. The highest-priority result will be broad acquaintance and involvement with symphonic music throughout the community affairs.
    a. In civic events.
    b. In sporting venues.
    c. In entertainment.
2. Second-highest priority will be inclusion of symphonic performances in public and private education.
3. The number of students of music will be higher than the national average.

POLICY TYPE: ENDS

POLICY TITLE: PURPOSE

Our community civic center purpose: *a culturally vibrant Lizaville.*

1. Strong cultural awareness, assigned no more than $200,000.
2. Vital downtown, assigned the greater priority of remaining resources.
    a. Strong cultural tourism, to be achieved even at the cost of b and c.
    b. Potent commercial activity.
    c. Healthy city image.
3. Effective partner organizations.
    a. Strong boards.
    b. Stable finances.

POLICY TYPE: ENDS

POLICY TITLE: MISSION AND PRIORITIES

The purpose of Hannahburg Hospital is *high quality, efficient remediation of disease and trauma conditions for no more than $185,000,000.*

1. Major focus is on the relief of acute conditions.
    a. All general med-surg conditions including emergencies.
    b. Restoration of physical functioning and maintenance of geriatric functioning no later than 1999; relief of acute psychiatric conditions, 2002.
2. Capability shall be sufficient for 80 percent of consumer needs in the metro area.
    a. The 20 percent of needs that do not have to be met includes burn and neonatal.
    b. For any health care needs not met, the product will be appropriate linkage with another provider whose outcomes are comparable to Hannahburg's.
3. Diagnostic knowledge (as a product) will be comprehensive, technologically advanced, and accessible.
    a. Diagnostic information available from cardiac testing and oncology will be the most reliable in the tristate area by no later than 2000.
    b. Diagnostic information available from imaging will be the most reliable in the tristate area by no later than 2001.
4. Geographical concentration will be on the Hannahburg metropolitan area.
5. Subsidy for health outcomes shall be no greater than 5 percent of gross revenues.
    a. First priority for subsidy will be given to life-threatening, emergency conditions.
    b. Other subsidy may be extended to Medicaid-Medicare patients.

POLICY TYPE: ENDS

POLICY TITLE: CONSUMER PRIORITIES

Consumers will be persons or families impaired by developmental disabilities and persons or families impaired by mental and emotional problems. Their relative proportions shall approximate the proportion of these disorders in the community.

1. With respect to those consumers impaired by developmental disabilities, approximately equal emphasis shall be placed on those who have (a) deficits in early infant stimulation, (b) deficits in independent living skills, (c) deficits in work skills, and (d) family stress due to the care of developmentally disabled persons. Expenditures on results (as specified in Ends policy "Results Priorities") for those with these needs shall be no less than 80 percent of developmental disabilities funds.

2. With respect to those consumers impaired by mental and emotional problems, no less than 45 percent of all expenditures shall be for persons who have (a) dysfunctions due to alcoholism and drug abuse, (b) family disorder due to presence or care of disturbed persons, (c) disturbance due to criminal attack or abuse, and (d) moderate emotional disturbance of whatever source.

3. With respect to those consumers impaired by mental and emotional problems, no less than 30 percent of expenditures shall be for those who have (a) living problems of the serious, chronically emotionally impaired, (b) acute reactions to life crises, (c) emotional dysfunction associated with criminality, and (d) lack of information about available services.

POLICY TYPE: ENDS

POLICY TITLE: RESULTS AND PRIORITIES

The mission of the Metropolitan Board of Realtors is enhanced demand for REALTOR services.

In pursuit of this mission, MBOR will bring about results in four areas:

1. Accurate and timely information and business tools for the conduct of REALTORS' business which shall, at minimum, include an MLS/Market Data Service and legal form for listing and selling real estate. This result is the highest priority of all results, with an applicable draw on MBOR resources.
2. The highest priority of the remaining results is a positive public image of REALTORS, where REALTORS are perceived as necessary to every real estate transaction.
3. A favorable environment for REALTORS' commerce in real estate, which shall be evidenced by laws, regulations, and public policy that:
    a. Accommodate and promote the growth of our metropolitan area.
    b. Encourage business expansion, new business investment, and the retention and creation of jobs.
    c. Facilitate and create freedom of choice in housing and equal access to affordable housing opportunities for all citizens.
    d. Minimize the constraints and costs associated with the ownership, use, improvement, and transfer of real property.
    e. Strengthen central area's position and image as an excellent place to live, work, and conduct business.
4. A highly skilled REALTOR membership.

Note: Our thanks to the Metropolitan Indianapolis Board of Realtors for the use of this policy. We have altered and abridged their actual document for purposes of illustration.

POLICY TYPE: ENDS

POLICY TITLE: CITY PRODUCTS

The global Ends of the City of Bryan is a healthy, safe, and successful community for a reasonable tax burden.

1.   People can move in, out, and within Bryan safely, quickly, and efficiently.
2.   Residents and visitors enjoy park space and recreational activities.
3.   Residents and visitors have reasonable protection from emergencies.
      a. Peace of mind and personal welfare.
      b. Low loss due to fire.
      c. Readiness for emergencies and natural disasters.
4.   Residents enjoy a modern and broad-based repository of information and knowledge.
5.   Economic life of the community is stable and appropriately growing.
      a. Adequate employment base.
      b. Diverse, recession-proof economy.
      c. A dynamic, positive business climate.
6.   Residents and visitors enjoy a safe environment.
      a. Adequate, high-quality drinking water.
      b. Efficient disposal of waste.
      c. Protection from flooding.
      d. Clean air.
      e. Adequate animal control and knowledge regarding the care of animals.
7.   Citizens enjoy an attractive, clean community.
      a. Attractive city and subdivision entrances.
      b. Controlled vegetation growth.
      c. No abandoned buildings.
      d. No junked vehicles.
8.   Adequate housing.

Note: Our thanks to the city council of Bryan, Texas, for the use of this policy. We have altered and abridged Bryan's actual document for purposes of illustration.

POLICY TYPE:	ENDS
POLICY TITLE:	PURPOSE AND OUTCOMES

The purpose of U.S. Cycling is *a dynamic and pervasive culture of cycling in America.* In order of priority, this purpose includes:

1. Widespread participation in fair and safe cycling activities for all ages, genders, and skill levels.
    a. A broad range of types of cycling, to include
        i.   Competition cycling with emphasis on track and time trialing.
        ii. Recreational cycling.
        iii. A broad range of participants, to include
             Opportunities for both genders with an emphasis on women.
             All ages with an emphasis on juniors, youth, and masters.
             A full spectrum of skill levels.
             Minorities.
2. Excellence in cycling competition, especially in elite juniors and seniors.
    a. In all competitions with an emphasis on international.
    b. Winning medals; placing in top eight in international events and in top three in UCI calendar events.
3. Widespread good public image of cycling.
4. Wide understanding of cycling information.
5. New knowledge of cycling science and sports medicine.

Note: Our thanks to U.S. Cycling for the use of this policy, which we have abridged for this illustration.

POLICY TYPE: ENDS

POLICY TITLE: PURPOSE

Erin Medical Research Institute exists for as much new information to reduce the human suffering and death caused by cancer as can reasonably be produced for $350,000,000 annually. Major components of this purpose are:

1. The highest-priority result will be basic knowledge of the chemical, molecular, and cellular microbiology of cancer.
    a. Understanding of why normal cells become cancerous.
        i. Understanding cellular responsiveness to normal regulatory factors.
            Response to receptors.
            Response to signal transductions.
            Response to second messengers.
        ii. Understanding molecular responsiveness to normal regulatory factors.
            Mutations of the gene itself.
            Factors that act upon the gene.
    b. Understanding the causes of growth and spread of cancer.
    c. Identification of factors that increase the risk of cancer.
    d. Discovery of genes that can prevent cancer.
2. The second-highest-priority result will be empirical methods by which laboratory findings can be made clinically applicable to the treatment and prevention of cancer.
    a. Effective clinical protocols for chemotherapy.
    b. Effective clinical protocols for radiation.
    c. Effective clinical protocols for hyperthermia.
3. Delivery technology capable of mitigating the psychological, social, spiritual, and economic effects of cancer on patients and their families.

Sample Monitoring Reports

We discussed monitoring in Chapter Six. In this Resource, we will illustrate several monitoring reports of the internal report type, that is, ones submitted to the board by the CEO. Monitoring reports in Policy Governance are rather straightforward documents, for they have a very straightforward task: merely to present whatever data concerning pre-stated criteria that would convince board members that a reasonable interpretation of those criteria has been achieved (in the case of Ends) or avoided (in the case of Executive Limitations).

Let us emphasize these points. Drifting away from them will substantially reduce the ability of a monitoring system to perform its critical function.

- The criteria are the words of the board's policies on Ends and Executive Limitations—not some additional requirement. In other words, the board does not have to concern itself with adding measurement methods.
- The data presented are only those that address the criteria being monitored—not a compendium of other data the CEO would like the board to know. This is very important in keeping the report lean, so that board members can never get lost in a flurry of information that does not constitute monitoring. Whatever the CEO would like the board to know (or, indeed, whatever information the board has asked to see) must be kept completely separate from the monitoring mechanism.
- Data means data. The monitoring report presents data that address the criteria, not just a statement by the CEO that criteria have been met.

• Because the monitoring report is always based on the words of board policy, we encourage the repetition of those words right in the report just to increase the ease for board members. Thus criteria and data are presented side by side.

Now let's look at several reports from a CEO to the board. These reports would have been in response to the board's chosen monitoring method (internal or CEO report in this case) and frequency. In order to illustrate monitoring reports, we have necessarily had to choose a format, though any number of formats will do. The important aspects, regardless of format, are that (1) the words of the applicable board policy are stated largely for convenience but also to focus board attention on its policy, as well as on the report, (2) the words themselves are treated as the criteria, and (3) the CEO assures the board with information that directly addresses the criteria rather than simply mere interest.

It is important for board peace of mind that the CEO signs for the global assessment, as well as for the validity of data submitted throughout the report. Regardless of format, it is crucial that the report be driven by the applicable board policy. The CEO does not submit a "report" that is defined apart from board policy. Balance sheets and income statements are examples of reports that are not criteria-driven.

Each example shown is of the internal report type (data gathered and submitted by the CEO). Keep in mind that monitoring reports are also available from outside resources, or by the board, or by a subpart of the board.

Internal Monitoring Report

POLICY TYPE: EXECUTIVE LIMITATIONS

POLICY TITLE: TREATMENT OF STAFF

GLOBAL POLICY PROHIBITION: *With respect to the treatment of paid and volunteer staff, the CEO may not cause or allow conditions that are unfair or undignified.* REPORT: This report constitutes my assurance that, as reasonably interpreted, these conditions have not occurred and further, that the data submitted below are accurate as of this date, April 15, 1999.
Signed_____, CEO

1. POLICY PROHIBITION: *Operate without written personnel policies that clarify the rules for staff, provide for effective handling of grievances, and protect against wrongful conditions, such as nepotism and grossly preferential treatment for personal reasons.* REPORT: Personnel policies affecting the entire organizational staff have been completed, with input from all interested parties. These policies contain protections against all of the conditions prohibited by board policy. A staff member recently hired on contract to complete Project Upstart is related by marriage to a senior manager in our organization. This hiring was completed without input from the manager in question. The hired person was the most skilled and experienced of the candidates. I am therefore reporting compliance.

2. POLICY PROHIBITION: *Discriminate against any staff for expressing an ethical dissent.* REPORT: This policy is interpreted to mean that staff must be able to freely express their disagreement with the organization's policies without fear of reprisals. It is also interpreted to mean that staff, while being free to disagree, may not refuse to work. A number of our staff disagree with the Ends policy adopted by the board that assigns a higher priority to female than to male indigent consumers. They are free to do so. An anonymous questionnaire administered by our state association in February demonstrated that 95 percent of our staff are sure that their dissent will not affect their employment in any way. This item from the survey report is attached. I am therefore reporting compliance.

3. POLICY PROHIBITION: *Prevent staff from grieving to the board when (a) internal grievance procedures have been exhausted and (b) the employee alleges that (c) board policy has been violated to his or her detriment, or (d) board policy does not protect his or her human rights.* REPORT: There have been no staff grievances that have been unresolved at the internal procedure level. I am therefore reporting compliance.

4. POLICY PROHIBITION: *Fail to acquaint staff with their rights under this policy.* REPORT: All new hires are provided with a copy of all board policies, and they sign a document acknowledging receipt of this. Further, on an annual basis, all staff are asked to read and acknowledge having read board policy, Treatment of Staff. I am therefore reporting compliance.

Internal Monitoring Report

POLICY TYPE:	EXECUTIVE LIMITATIONS
POLICY TITLE:	FINANCIAL CONDITION AND ACTIVITIES

GLOBAL POLICY PROHIBITION: *With respect to the actual, ongoing financial condition and activities, the CEO shall not cause or allow the development of fiscal jeopardy or a material deviation of actual expenditures from board priorities established in board Ends policies.* REPORT: This report constitutes my assurance that, as reasonably interpreted, these conditions have not occurred *except as shown,* and further that the data submitted below are accurate as of this date, April 15, 1999. VIOLATION: Board Ends policies place a high (that is, 60 percent resources) priority on safe housing. A fire in one of our safe houses has resulted in its temporary closure. Alternatives to this means are being brought into action, but as of this date, expenditures for this result area are below criterion. This violation is reported, along with my assurance that performance in line with board priorities will be restored in two weeks.
Signed_____, CEO

1. POLICY PROHIBITION: *Expend more funds than have been received in the fiscal year to date unless the debt guideline (to follow) is met.* REPORT: To date, the agency has received a total of $3,643,254 and spent $2,874,831. I am therefore reporting compliance.

2. POLICY PROHIBITION: *Indebt the organization in an amount greater than can be repaid by certain, otherwise unencumbered revenue within sixty days.* REPORT: No indebtedness has been incurred. I am therefore reporting compliance.

3. POLICY PROHIBITION: *Use any long-term reserves.* REPORT: The funds designated as long-term reserves by your auditors were reported at a level of $368,000 at last year's end. They are now worth $369,500, the increase being due to accumulated interest. These funds are not used by anyone other than the board. I am therefore reporting compliance.

4. POLICY PROHIBITION: *Conduct interfund shifting in amounts greater than can be restored to a condition of discrete fund balances by certain, otherwise unencumbered revenues within thirty days.* REPORT: I have used general funds to secure temporary replacement safe housing for our female indigent consumers, since funds designated for such cannot be used while the shelter is under repair. These funds can be replaced in the month following rehousing of our consumers, according to state law. Hence interfund borrowing has occurred, but I am expecting the righting of this borrowing to be complete within the time period allowed by board policy. I am therefore reporting compliance.

5. POLICY PROHIBITION: *Fail to settle payroll and debts in a timely manner.* REPORT: I interpret "timely" to mean, in the case of payroll, on the morning of every other Thursday. Payroll issue has not missed this deadline. For other payables, I interpret "timely" to mean within sixty days. One invoice was not paid within sixty days of its receipt, since appropriate paperwork was not sent with it. Undisputed debts have been paid within sixty days. I am therefore reporting compliance.

6. POLICY PROHIBITION: *Allow tax payments or other government-ordered payments to be overdue or inaccurately filed.* REPORT: All withholding taxes and other such payments have been made within

deadline. There are no outstanding filings or late penalties. I am therefore reporting compliance.

7. POLICY PROHIBITION: *Make a single purchase or commitment of greater than $45,000.* REPORT: No purchase of such a size has been made. I am reporting compliance.

8. POLICY PROHIBITION: *Acquire, encumber, or dispose of real property.* REPORT: The organization has made no changes in its property holdings. I am therefore reporting compliance.

9. POLICY PROHIBITION: *Fail to aggressively pursue receivables after a reasonable grace period.* REPORT: While there are a number of outstanding receivables in respect to our recent fund-raising gala, we are expecting that these will be settled within a month. These were pursued after a one-month delay. Client receivables, usually user fees, are pursued but after a two-month delay. I am therefore reporting compliance.

Internal Monitoring Report

POLICY TYPE: ENDS

POLICY TITLE: MEMBER BENEFITS

GLOBAL POLICY: *The purpose of the Provincial Psychological Association is that members enjoy circumstances necessary for successful practice.* REPORT: Along with more specific queries (see #1 and #2 following) in the weeks just prior to April 15, 1999, members were asked to rate their perception of the extent to which this global situation is the case for them. Eighty percent answered either "adequately" or "thoroughly true" on a 5-point scale. Fewer than 10 percent responded "totally untrue" or "mostly untrue." Along with the data to follow, I offer these data as demonstration of having attained a reasonable interpretation of the global policy provision.
Signed_____, CEO

1. POLICY PROVISION: *Members will have the skills and information necessary for profitable and ethical office operation.* REPORT: My inter-

pretation of "skills necessary for profitable operation" is the basic skills of small-office financial record keeping, personnel management, and billing practices. My interpretation of "information necessary for ethical operation" is that each member has at hand an up-to-date handbook of standards of professional conduct. Between March 15 and April 1, a randomly chosen group of fifty members were interviewed by telephone to ascertain their assessment of whether, in their opinion, each of these skills and resources is either reasonably in their grasp or already achieved. The results of that survey are that the following percentages of members queried agree that success in their opinion has been achieved: financial record keeping, 80 percent; personnel management, 90 percent; billing practices, 60 percent; standards of conduct, 100 percent. While the billing practices rating is low (and is being addressed now), the average percentage is such that I submit that performance is a reasonable interpretation of the policy requirement.

2. POLICY PROVISION: *Legislators will have reasonable acquaintance with members' issues with respect to impending or desirable legislation.* REPORT: My interpretation is that whatever constitutes a "reasonable acquaintance" is greater among relevant health committee legislators than among other legislators. I assembled a group of five knowledgeable association members and asked that they determine the five most important facts about, or positions of, practicing psychologists, with respect to legislation or potential legislative initiatives. I then talked with each health committee legislator's legislative aide and with ten randomly chosen legislators who are not on that committee. I averaged the "awareness" of legislators across all five facts-positions, with the results as follows: health committee legislators' aides had a surprisingly high awareness of 92 percent; other legislators averaged 65 percent. I submit that these findings constitute a reasonable interpretation of the policy provision.

3. POLICY PROVISION: *Members will know the status of legislative issues, with particular priority given to issues of substantial import to the profession.* REPORT: Each association member receives a monthly legislative update in summary form, easy and quick to read, plus faxed updates at times of rapid legislative movement. This illustrates accessibility of information but does not fully address

whether members "know the status. . . ." To ascertain the level of knowledge, twenty members at random were called and asked if they were aware of the general status of two current legislative issues. Only five answered such that I could claim they reasonably met the requirement of the policy provision. Therefore, I must report a POLICY VIOLATION with respect to this result. I am casting about for ways to change methods, but I may return to the board with information that suggests the result is perhaps unattainable. If so, that would likely be due more to lack of members' motivation to know such matters until they are personally affected than to whether the information is easily accessible to them.

4. POLICY PROVISION: *The public views the profession as ethical, effective, and accessible.* REPORT: My interpretation of "views the profession as ethical" is that the general public, with particular attention to the ordinary referral sources, sees psychologists as trustworthy with confidences and with billing matters. My interpretation of "views . . . as . . . effective" is that the same population sees psychologists as capable of dealing with moderate and severe emotional disorders and problems, as well as problems with relationships (excluding situations requiring medication). My interpretation of "views . . . as . . . accessible" is that the same population sees psychologists as easy to find (in the Yellow Pages, for example) and personally approachable (not intimidating). To assess these characteristics, I requested that one hundred persons complete the experimental "Professional Perceptions" questionnaire developed by the Department of Statistical Analysis at Clynie University. Half of the one hundred persons are from five common referral sources (schools, hospitals, public health department, health practitioners, pastoral care), and the remainder were randomly chosen from adult students at the community college. To our pleasure, psychologists ranked quite high (85 percent "high approval") on a conglomerate of the characteristics included in the board policy, higher than general medical practitioners, lawyers, and accountants, though slightly lower than psychiatric social workers and clergy on the same measures. I would argue that this finding demonstrates a reasonable interpretation of the policy provision.

Internal Monitoring Report

POLICY TYPE: EXECUTIVE LIMITATIONS

POLICY TITLE: FINANCIAL PLANNING

GLOBAL POLICY PROHIBITION: *In budgeting for any portion of a fiscal year, the CEO shall not jeopardize intended Ends proportions or fiscal integrity.* REPORT: I submit that the data to follow demonstrate compliance with this global provision; further I add my personal certification and guarantee that, as reasonably interpreted, this provision has not been violated up to and as of this date, April 15, 1999.
Signed_____, CEO

1. POLICY PROHIBITION: *Budgeting is not acceptable that contains too little detail to enable reasonably accurate projection of revenues and expenses, separation of capital and operational items, cash flow, and a basis for subsequent audit trails.* REPORT: Projections of revenues and expenses are built on assumptions screened by a multidisciplinary process that for the past three years has had an accuracy of plus-or-minus 3 percent in six-month projections. Capital and operational items are treated separately. A separate cash flow plan is calculated and updated quarterly. The budgeting contains the same amount of detail and subsequent audit trail traceability found sufficient by the auditor for the last three years.

2. POLICY PROHIBITION: *Budgeting is unacceptable that plans to expend in any fiscal year more funds than are conservatively projected to be received in that period.* REPORT: Expenditures planned for the remainder of the current fiscal year are $6,700,000 out of revenues of $7,200,000. My interpretation of "conservatively" is based on (1) timing and (2) certainty. Timing of all revenue receipts in each category of revenue is projected as the slowest of all receipts in the applicable category during the past three years. Certainty of projection is attained by counting at 100 percent all revenues under contract from established sources. Contracted amounts from sources with which we have no track record are counted at 80

percent. Noncontracted sources are carried at the percentage found to be actual in the past five years. No matter how certain or uncertain, however, all projected revenues are counted at 100 percent so long as the expenditures that depend on those amounts are still distant enough to be postponed or canceled without substantial programmatic disruption.

3. POLICY PROHIBITION: *Financial planning is unacceptable if its projected effect is to reduce current assets at any time to less than twice current liabilities.* REPORT: Current assets at their lowest are expected to be $142,004 in mid June. Current liabilities at their highest are expected to be $75,300 in late May. Should these high and low points be approximated at an overlapping time period, however, the current ratio will be as low as 1.89:1. Therefore, there is a FAIR PROBABILITY OF VIOLATION of this policy for a period not to exceed three weeks in May or June.

4. POLICY PROHIBITION: *Financial planning is unacceptable that deviates materially from board-stated priorities in its allocation among competing result areas.* REPORT: Budget categories, as related to funding by result areas, are no more than 2 percent deviant from board priorities stated in Ends policies. I refer you to my monitoring report on your Priorities of Results policy for my interpretation of your policy language in allocation percentages and dollar amounts.

4. POLICY PROHIBITION: *Financial planning is unacceptable if it violates or reasonably can be expected to lead to violation of generally accepted accounting practices, except when alternate methods are required by funding sources.* REPORT: I have been assured both by the internal auditor and by the external auditor's representative that no such violation exists (see letters attached).

Selected Readings

Because Policy Governance is a new technology of governance—a departure from the long-standing, conventional wisdom—the number of authoritative resources about it are still few. In other words, Policy Governance is a whole new game. Reading the current literature about an old game will not help you much.

Consequently, for some years there will be a paucity of good governance guidance with the model integrity that Policy Governance calls for. While this is unfortunate, it is the normal course of nature when new paradigms are first spread. The following list is not complete, but it contains the most available, model-consistent literature at press time.

In reading literature that is not model-consistent, you must be extremely careful to extract the wisdom you find there in such a way that your governance integrity is not damaged. This can be done in some cases, but requires acute attention to what does and does not fit the model.

The following resources are all model-consistent with Policy Governance. The *Board Leadership* special issues are a select few among more than thirty issues published as this text goes to press. A complete list of all publications is available from the authors or from the following Web site: http://carvergovernance.com.

Carver, J. *Boards That Make a Difference: A New Design for Leadership in Non-profit and Public Organizations.* San Francisco: Jossey-Bass, 1990.

Carver, J. *Empowering Boards for Leadership: Redefining Excellence in Governance.* Audiocassette program. San Francisco: Jossey-Bass, 1992.

Carver, J. *Board Leadership*, 1993, *6*, 1–12. [special fiduciary issue].

Carver, J. *Board Leadership,* 1993, *10,* 1–12. [special board self-evaluation issue].

Carver, J. *John Carver on Board Governance.* Videocassette program. San Francisco: Jossey-Bass, 1993.

Carver, J. *Board Leadership,* 1995, *18,* 1–11. [special ownership issue].

Carver, J. "The 'Any Reasonable Interpretation' Rule: Leap of Faith or Sine Qua Non of Delegation?" *Board Leadership,* 1996, *28,* 1–5.

Carver, J. *Board Leadership,* 1996, *26,* 1–12. [special evaluation of the CEO issue].

Carver, J. *The Chairperson's Role as Servant-Leader to the Board.* CarverGuide Series, No. 4. San Francisco: Jossey-Bass, 1996.

Carver, J. *Creating a Mission That Makes a Difference.* CarverGuide Series, No. 6. San Francisco: Jossey-Bass, 1996.

Carver, J. *Planning Better Board Meetings.* CarverGuide Series, No. 5. San Francisco: Jossey-Bass, 1996.

Carver, J. *Three Steps to Fiduciary Responsibility.* CarverGuide Series, No. 3. San Francisco: Jossey-Bass, 1996.

Carver, J. *Board Assessment of the CEO.* CarverGuide Series, No. 7. San Francisco: Jossey-Bass, 1997.

Carver, J. *Board Self-Assessment.* CarverGuide Series, No. 8. San Francisco: Jossey-Bass, 1997.

Carver, J., and Mayhew Carver, M. *A New Vision of Board Leadership: Governing the Community College.* Washington, D.C.: Association of Community College Trustees, 1994.

Carver, J., and Mayhew Carver, M. *Basic Principles of Policy Governance.* CarverGuide Series, No. 1. San Francisco: Jossey-Bass, 1996.

Carver, J., and Mayhew Carver, M. *Making Diversity Meaningful in the Boardroom.* CarverGuide Series, No. 9. San Francisco: Jossey-Bass, 1996.

Carver, J., and Mayhew Carver, M. *Your Roles and Responsibilities as a Board Member.* CarverGuide Series, No. 2. San Francisco: Jossey-Bass, 1996.

Royer, G. *School Board Leadership 2000: The Things Staff Didn't Tell You at Orientation.* Houston: Brockton, 1996.

Index